ENDORSEMENTS

Leif Hetland has been a personal friend for many years. We have ministered together on numerous occasions, and I have been profoundly impacted by the principles he put in his new book, *Called to Reign*. He brings the believer back to the foundational truth of what it means to live a life full of purpose and fulfillment, which can only happen as we learn to live from a place of rest. Ripe with revelation, *Called to Reign* is a powerful catalyst to uproot the lies often created by anemic religious systems, and it helps to pave the way for discovering our calling or purpose in life. This book is powerful! It is powerful enough to affect how we think, while bringing greater freedom into every reader's life!

Bill Johnson
Pastor of Bethel Church, Redding, CA
Author of *When Heaven Invades Earth* and *God Is Good*

Leif Hetland is an anointed communicator and a friend. His new book, *Called to Reign*, brings a vital message for the church. Filled with foundational teaching on identity, intimacy, inheritance, and destiny, this book will bless you as it calls you to come up higher and reign from the place of rest close to the heart of God.

Dr. Randy Clark
Founder and President of Global Awakening & the Apostolic
Network of Global Awakening
Author of *Baptized in the Spirit, Authority to Heal,* and
Healing Breakthrough

Leif Hetland is an amazing hero of the faith. He steps out where others fear to go. His newest book, *Called to Reign* acknowledges the critical condition of the 'church' challenging believers to reign as 'kingdom bringers.' Leif offers a powerful and heartfelt roadmap for followers of Jesus to find peace, rest and ultimately, what we all really want… intimacy with the Father. The concept of 'love' is more than just an impractical sounding cliché; I have witnessed the strategy that Leif advocates work miracles even amongst religious radicals and dictators. His tactic of love, compassion and mercy really does work to bring reconciliation in even the most extreme circumstances. If followers of Jesus were to operate in Leif's kingdom mindset by living daily in the 'love language' of heaven, it would change the world as we know it. In this generation of fear, deception and division, followers of Jesus must be known as 'Ambassadors of Love' - this is how we are called to reign.

Mark Siljander
U.S. Congressman, U.S./U.N. Ambassador (ret)
Author of *A Deadly Misunderstanding* & *President of Bridges*
to Common Ground

Leif Hetland is a dear friend of mine and also a friend of God. He is passionate to see God's Kingdom come, and ready for any assignment no matter how radical. Leif's book, *Called to Reign*, is about understanding who we are as sons and daughters of our loving and tender daddy God. We are loved unconditionally before we ever do a thing. When we stay in this place of resting in God, knowing who we are and knowing we have access to the resources of heaven, we can dream big dreams for others and ourselves; we can shift atmospheres and carry God's glory on the earth. Read this book and allow God to heal every false mindset and pour His liquid love into your heart. You are called to reign!

Heidi G. Baker, PhD
Co-Founder and CEO of Iris Global

In 2019 I complete 70 years of ordained ministry and can say without hesitation that one of the brightest moments in my entire career was when I met Leif Hetland and established the father/son relationship we now share. Today, I hold in my hand his monumental work, *Called to Reign*; a literary confirmation of his amazing ministry. In it, Leif reveals the Holy Spirit's awesome intent that every disciple of Jesus is "called to reign!" If I, and a million other young pastors, had been given this book the day we were ordained the history of the church would be far different!

Charles Carrin
Author, Christian Evangelist

Over the years I've had the privilege of meeting many leaders in the body of Christ from many different denominations and Leif Hetland is truly one of the most unique. I have never seen a combination of both power and childlikeness functioning in anyone as I've seen in Leif. In *Called to Reign,* Leif shares with us the priceless treasures he has received directly from heaven; treasures of revelation that carry the substance to transform our souls into gold - emanating the brightest light to the world around us.

Absolutely nothing in all of creation should matter more to us than nurturing and growing our intimate relationship with the Father, Jesus and Holy Spirit. For knowing God *is* eternal life as Jesus teaches us in John 17:3. Leif Hetland has a strong anointing to help lead the body into deeper intimacy with God. I implore anyone and everyone to follow Leif Hetland into the pages of this book and allow him to take you by the hand as you drink in every word of *Called to Reign.*

Brian "Head" Welch
Co-founder of Korn and *New York Times* best-selling author
of *Save Me From Myself*, as well as *Stronger* and *With My*
Eyes Wide Open

As a young Christian, "reigning in life" was something we would all do in the future, in The Millennium. However, Leif Hetland challenges us to believe that God still loves the world, even our enemies! He contends that we best accomplish our co-mission with Jesus by coming to the amazing place of rest where His yoke is easy!

Bishop Joseph L. Garlington Sr.
Reconciliation! A Network of Churches and Ministries

"Are you receiving all God has for you? Are you at heavenly rest and peace in your life, in all areas? Most believers cannot say, "yes." This book is a "how to." I call it "how to be normal based on the Word of God."

Sid Roth
Host, *It's Supernatural!*

Leif and his wife Jennifer have been friends of ours for over 10 years. I remember well the very first time I witnessed the three chairs. I am delighted that this teaching is now in a book. Leif enables us all to learn from our successes and our failures, to pick ourselves up and get back in the right chair. I can visualize him teach as I read, and that means that the book makes me smile. Leif is a man of faith and great generosity, giving himself away in every season and every place he goes, and now he is increasing that gift through the pages of this book. His desire will become yours - to find rest in this world and in the Father. The first time I met Leif he was a guest speaker, and now he is our friend. My wife Sue and I will never forget serving him. It gives me great pleasure to endorse this book written by such a great speaker and a dear friend because I know that it is not the result of preparing to speak a great message, but the pursuit of living a great life.

Paul Manwaring
Bethel Church, Redding, CA
Author of *Kisses from a Good God* and *What on Earth Is Glory*

Called to Reign is a must-read book for those who desire deeper experiences with God and to live out the abundant and victorious life He has promised for all of His children. In every page, Leif Hetland, my spiritual father, shares the gold nuggets of revelations and wisdom that he has received in the secret place with the Father and faithfully stewarded through the years of pouring God's love to the nations bringing healing, salvation and transformation. I have had the privilege of joining him on a number of ministry trips to some of the most spiritually dark regions of the world, and I have personally witnessed how he carries and releases the presence of God that shifts spiritual atmospheres resulting in massive healings, miracles and transformations. While there are some simple and practical steps mentioned in this book that are very helpful, this is not "how-to" material. In these pages you will find stories and revelations that serve as a guiding light that gives understanding and wisdom to our walk as beloved sons and daughters ruling and reigning in life. I highly recommend this book to leaders and fathers of movements, and churches and cultures who desire to raise up a people compelled and empowered by the love of God to bring heaven to earth in all arenas of life.

Paul P. Yadao
Senior Pastor, Destiny Ministries International, Philippines
Spiritual son of Leif Hetland

In his book, *Called to Reign*, Leif Hetland has captured the heart of Jesus' call to: "come and learn from Me" (Matthew 11:25 – 30). Jesus describes His life as coming out of intimacies and knowledge of a Father and Son relationship and that He is ready to go over it line by line with anyone willing to listen.

Leif, over many decades, has listened carefully to Jesus about practical ways we can all put into place to recover Christian spirituality so that we walk and work with Jesus from a Kingdom perspective. He provides us with the tools to act upon Eugene Peterson's powerful interpretation: "…watch how I do it. Learn the unforced rhythms of grace."

As you read *Called to Reign* you will be empowered to join a worldwide move of the Spirit to play your part in ushering in the Kingdom of God.

Peter McHugh
Stairway Church, Melbourne, Australia

When I first heard Leif preach on the content of this book, I knew that the message was one that the Church so desperately needs to hear. In my relationship with Leif, most of our conversations revolve around the idea that true breakthrough in the Kingdom only comes through deep rest in the Father's heart. Leif has been given a revelation from the Father on the power of rest in the life of His children. Through

Leif's metaphor of the 'Three Chairs' we see that ordinary people can learn extraordinary strategy from heaven on the principle of actually working from a place of rest. You will find that this book will help you connect to God and learn the rhythms of what He deems normal. I bless you in the name of Jesus Christ with the ability to take the principles of Leif's revelation and to step more fully into your own identity and eventual destiny.

Chad Norris
Lead Pastor of Bridgeway Church, Greenville, SC

Leif Hetland is a dear covenant friend and partner in ministry who carries a deep realm of truth and revelation. As I read the pages of his new book, *Called to Reign* my heart was deeply moved by the words I read because I believe they came directly from the Father's heart. Leif has constantly demonstrated what a life of love and intimacy with God looks like. *Called to Reign* will change your thinking, transform your heart, renew your mind, and awaken you to the Father's love as you read each sentence. I have listened to Leif preach, watched him minister with pure love and joy, and live from a place of resting in God. Over the years I've been greatly blessed as I have had the honor of watching Leif live out the pages of this book. It is refreshing and empowering to watch someone live what they are preaching, teaching, and writing about. As you read this book, I believe that you will receive an impartation and a deep deposit of truth and love that flow from a lifetime of Leif's encounters, revelation, and personal testimony. My heart has been so refreshed by the Father's love through this book that was written from a place of love and transparency. I highly recommend and encourage every pastor, leader, minister, and believer to read *Called to Reign*. It will definitely change your life.

David Wagner
Fathers Heart Ministries, Pensacola, Florida

CALLED TO
REIGN

LIVING AND LOVING FROM A PLACE OF REST

LEIF HETLAND

FOREWORD BY KRIS VALLOTTON

CALLED TO REIGN

Global Mission Awareness
Copyright 2017-Leif Hetland

This book and all of Leif Hetland's books are available at Christian bookstores and distributors worldwide.

Cover design by Yvonne Parks | www.pearcreative.ca
Interior design by Nick Wallace | Reddovedesign.com
Publisher: Convergence Press

CON\/ERGENCEPRESS

Hardcover ISBN-13: 978-1947165014
Paperback ISBN-13: 978-1947165632
eBook ISBN-13: 978-1947165342

Global Mission Awareness on the web: https://globalmissionawareness.com/

DEDICATION

My life is dedicated to seeing the 7.5 billion people on earth having an experience of how good Papa God is and how loved each one of them are.

This book is dedicated to my spiritual parents Papa Jack and Mama Friede Taylor. Your love for Jesus, His kingdom and for me is transformational. I also dedicate this life message to Paul and Ahlmira Yadao and the family of Destiny Ministries International in the Philippines. As a spiritual son, daughter and family, you have taught me to discover the destiny in my identity as a son.

The Kingdom Family Movement is unstoppable! We are all *called to reign* together with Him as a family on mission!

ACKNOWLEDGMENTS

A book is never written by an author without the history, heart and hands of contributors and influencers in their life. My wife and best friend Jennifer is the greatest gift given to me—a gift that never stops giving. Our children Leif Emmanuel, Laila, Courtney, and Katherine, and our son-in-law RayVon continue to give me the passion and purpose to fulfill my potential as they live love to the world around them.

I want to thank my Executive Director Scott Wilson and my team at Global Mission Awareness for your spirit and pursuit of excellence as you continue to make me look better than I am. Thank you to David Edwards, Paul Yadao and my daughter Laila, for your diligence and contribution in developing the framework and content of this manuscript. I am grateful to Chris Tiegreen and Susan Thompson for your invaluable ability to convey the depth of my thought and the passion of my heart without losing my voice in the process. Finally, I thank you Holy Spirit, my best friend, for guiding me through the years of process to entrust my life with this message for your family.

CONTENTS

PREFACE

by Dr. Jack Taylor
President of *Dimension Ministries* and
Founder of *Sonslink, a Kingdom Family Connection*

Leif Hetland is a spiritual son of mine who has taught me much about fathering, as well as what it means to be a son. He is a devoted son with a sonship characterized by avid pursuit and constant communication mixed with the language of love.

I choose books to read based on two criteria: first, on the basis of my knowledge of the author and his or her credibility, and second, on the basis of the title. I then ask questions such as "Is it pertinent? Is it relevant? "Is it" timely? Is it anointed?" If the answers are positive, the urgency to read the book becomes a major factor and, in time, a living experience. Leif Hetland's *Called to Reign*, not only meets these criteria; it exceeds them!

Each and every one of us is either reigning or being reigned over. We have no trouble reigning over comfortable conditions, pleasant responsibilities and encouraging circumstances. But, when that peacefulness is disturbed we often crash and burn, forgetting that victory implies conflict, pain and struggle that demand intentional responses on our part. In the pages of this book, Leif is calling us to face the challenges of all of life's demands – the good, the bad and the ugly – and reign over them. The richest among us are those who are learning to take everything that happens and, through patient obedience, allow God to transform it and us into messages of encouragement to the watching world. This is precisely what we behold in the greatest life ever lived, the greatest death ever died and the greatest victory ever achieved, i.e., our Savior, the Lord Jesus Christ. Through Him we are challenged to reign.

Since by one man's trespass, death reigned through that one man, how much more will those who receive the overflow of grace and the gift of righteousness reign in life through the one man Jesus Christ.

Romans 5:16 HCSB

Leif Hetland is a man who is learning to reign then reporting back to others with instructions, incentives and testimonies to help us along the way. Thank you Leif, for leaning your heart toward us and guiding us by the light God has entrusted to you. I'll sign off now as you always encourage me to do . . .

Singing in the Reign
Jack Taylor

P.S. When something happens and you don't know what to do with the circumstances swirling around you, just "rein" them in and "reign" over them. It's definitely more fun than being stomped!

FOREWORD

Senior Associate Leader, Bethel Church, Redding, CA

Co-founder of the Bethel School of Supernatural Ministry

Author of thirteen books, including *The Supernatural Ways of Royalty*

and *Destined to Win*

I've noticed that most of our society is struggling with a major identity crisis. A lot of people don't know what they're supposed to be doing with their lives. Society has created a cycle of striving as we succumb to the pressures of picking a major in college, choosing the "right" career path, finding the "perfect" job. In the end we're spinning our wheels to find undiscovered meaning. Spinout turns to burnout, an all-too-familiar term, and its prevalence is a sign of the church losing our grip on the reality of life with Jesus. The underlying message in these decisions is that finding our life purpose and mission is in what we choose to do with our lives. The idea of discovering our calling isn't a bad one, but the breakdown in truth happens when we define our identities by what we do, not who we are.

The truth is that we are not mere victims to a performance-driven culture. Striving comes from a lack of identity and is relegated to the children of a lesser god. It is the condition of slaves who have yet to discover their freedom on the other side of the river of baptism. The truth is that with His blood, Jesus purchased ragged sinners and re-created us into His righteous, reigning saints. We are no longer orphans striving for meaning and purpose, but sons and daughters of the living King! We were made to be vessels of His glory and reigning vehicles of His light!

In this incredible book, Leif Hetland prescribes an antidote for burnout: true rest that can only be found in a solid identity in Christ. He creates space in these pages for encounters with a loving Father, empowering us to go from simply knowing about God to ruling and reigning with Him. My favorite part about this book is the clarity Leif brings by teaching us the divine order of reigning with God: first, understanding our identity as one's who belong to the King of the world; second, diving into intimacy with the Lord and learning to truly walk with Him every day; third, taking ownership of our inheritance and living as co-heirs with Christ; and finally, soaring into our destinies as we're launched from a foundation of royalty!

Called to Reign could not come at a better time in history. I believe that everyone who reads it will walk away transformed to impact the world around them from a place of divine rest!

INTRODUCTION

One of my favorite ways to illustrate humanity's worldviews is to put three chairs on a stage to represent three kinds of people. The picture for this began when I was ministering in a large African-American church in Alabama. The presence was strong, and healing began to break loose. It was a powerful impartation. I remember being very overwhelmed by God's faithfulness as many people experienced breakthrough from Jesus' touch. After the service, as I sat in the car to begin my 30-minute drive home, I thought, "Wow, that was powerful this morning. Leif, you were really anointed." I felt so good about that. But in a few moments, I felt as if the presence had lifted. I was scheduled to return for the evening service, and as I thought about it, I was crippled with fear. Someone called to let me know that because of the powerful service that morning, some were planning to bring people in great need to the evening service—people in wheelchairs or with Down Syndrome, people who were in institutions, people from all walks of life who needed a creative miracle. The faith level of this congregation had gone up, but I just felt overwhelmed by the pressure.

All the way home, I was praying in the Spirit to get His peace and presence back, but it never came. That afternoon, I tried to soak, pray in the Spirit, anything I could think of, but nothing happened. One moment the Dove had been there in the car with me; the next moment He was gone. Why did He leave? How had the environment shifted from an open heaven to being closed off from His presence? Suddenly I realized the pride in my thoughts—how I had started to think about what I had done instead of what Jesus had done. As I rehearsed the service in my mind, I realized there was absolutely nothing I had done to create that environment. It was all God. As soon as I began thinking it was me, I moved out of the place of anointing. Now it felt like me against the giants. It was one of the most awful feelings in the world.

In that moment, the thought came to me, "Leif, what chair are you sitting in?" I got a picture of having moved from one chair to another, and I knew I needed to be back in that chair I had been sitting in that morning. My resting and reigning depended on it. I repented, and I went back to the church that evening with a different attitude. *Without Him I can do nothing, but with Him I can do all things in Christ who strengthens me.* I was no longer afraid of facing the giants in there. My confidence was in Him.

That was my starting point for this illustration of three chairs. At the time, I only pictured two chairs—resting and reigning in the Spirit, and striving independently of Him. But a journey began and a language for this image developed. I began to understand how easy it is for believers to move between Chair 1 and Chair 2 with just a comment, a thought, a criticism, or a correction from someone. A simple shift in attitude makes a huge difference in how we are resting in the Dove and reigning with Jesus.

Since then, I've seen three-chair illustrations used in different messages over the years by Tommy Barnett, John Maxwell, Bruce Wilkinson, and perhaps some others, and it creates a powerful picture. My message is quite a bit different from others, but I build on this illustration because it makes such a powerful point. Now, when I am teaching on this, I set up three chairs on the stage and say that out of the seven-plus billion people in the world, every single one of them is living his or her life from one of these chairs. Chair 1 is about the kingdom of God, Chair 2 is the kingdom of self, and Chair 3 is the kingdom of the world.

CHAIR 1 – ROOTED IN SONSHIP

In Chair 1, you realize the kingdom is not about the things of this world, so your focus is never on problems but always on kingdom opportunities.

Christians are in Chairs 1 and 2. If you are living in either of those chairs, you are saved. But there are many differences between Chair 1 and Chair 2. Most Christians live from Chair 2, even if they have visited Chair 1 at times. Chair 1 is a beautiful place to be. Those who live from that place are rooted in the spirit of sonship, which we talk about quite a bit in this book. Chair 1 is about experiencing God's pleasure without ever having to perform. In fact, you already have an A+ on your report card before you ever go out and do something. In Chair 1, you live from a place of total acceptance and rest. The Dove, the Holy Spirit, comes to rest on you; you become His habitation. You can hear the Father's voice as a son or daughter and trust that He is able to guide you. You know you belong, so you can believe God's promises and then behave as He has called you to do—you learn to put "be," "have," and "do" in the right order. You know who you are and then you live from your inheritance and walk out your destiny. You aren't just trying to get from earth to heaven but also want to bring heaven to earth. You can live as a river overflowing righteousness, peace, and joy in the Spirit (Romans 14:17), overwhelmed with the things of God, because that is the atmosphere of the kingdom.

CHAIR 2 – THE KINGDOM OF SELF

In Chair 2, you have a tendency to live *for* God rather than living *from* God because you have become rooted in the orphan spirit rather than a spirit of sonship.

Chair 2 is the kingdom of self. Most people don't think Chair 2 describes their worldview because they don't recognize the subtle differences. We have all been Chair 2 Christians at times, and we can easily slip from Chair 1 into Chair 2 thinking at any point in our lives. But over time, we learn to see the difference. You are always under pressure to perform because it's what you do that makes you who you are. You experience the Holy Spirit's visitation but not His habitation as the Dove resting on you. Instead of confidently hearing God's voice, you try to discern His will while fearing you might be misled by the self or the devil. Instead of being a son or daughter in order to have and then to do, Chair 2 believers are trying to believe the right way in order to behave the right way in order to belong. You try to live from inheritance and destiny so you can know who you are rather than the other way around. You're always trying to become something because you don't know or have forgotten your true identity. You're trying to get to heaven rather than trying to bring heaven to earth.

Chair 2 Christians often talk about how bad things are getting and how God's judgment is coming on this problem or that city. They are like the disciples who wanted to call down judgment on a Samaritan town that did not receive Jesus (Luke 9:54). Jesus rebuked them because He came to bring life not destroy it. Those in Chair 2 are both afraid of the world and influenced by it because the perspective is that if you don't separate from the world, you will be corrupted by it. If you touch a leper, literally or figuratively, you become unclean. Everything in Chair 2 is rooted in fear, even when it is disguised in the vocabulary of love.

I am convinced that much of the church is living from Chair 2 and doing ministry from that perspective—not motivated by love but by fear. They serve not because of their significance as sons and daughters in the kingdom but in order to become someone significant in the kingdom. They work not *from* God but *for* Him. Hundreds of thousands of churches are filled with Chair 2 people who know about the Father but don't actually find their identity in Him or make their home in His living room. They function as spiritual orphanages.

The Chair 2 perspective is always thinking about self. *Why didn't I get blessed the way that other person did? Lord, what are You going to do for me?* Once when Lenny LeBlanc and I were ministering together, I adapted his beautiful worship song "There Is None Like You" into a Chair 2 version: "There Is None Like Me"! That's the focus of a Chair 2 position. I've had people tell me they came to hear me speak but didn't like having to sit through two hours of worship. "That's okay," I say. "It wasn't for you. It was for Him." An orphan spirit says, "I didn't get what I needed! Where is it!?" For many of us, Chair 2 has become normal, but it is actually abnormal in the kingdom. Jesus is normal. In the kingdom, anything that does not look like Him is not.

CHAIR 3 – LOST

If you are living in Chair 3, you are lost. That is the world system apart from Jesus, outside of the kingdom of God. It includes 1.6 billion Muslims, more than a billion Hindus, and nearly half a billion Buddhists, as well as atheists, agnostics, and every other non-Christian.[1] Every one of these people is looking for love, security, value, significance, and purpose; it's in our DNA as human beings. But they aren't able to find these things, whether they are looking in religion, money, accomplishments, or anything else. I believe the biggest god in

---

1 https://joshuaproject.net

the world right now is money, regardless of the religion of the people seeking it. Whatever people serve, that's what they worship.

RETURN TO YOUR FIRST LOVE

The move from Chair 1 to Chair 2 often happens across generations. The church at Ephesus was in Chair 1—revival, open heavens, signs and wonders. By the time of Revelation, that church had left its first love (Revelation 2:4). In the generations after the New Testament, they didn't believe in God at all. You see this pattern today in institutions like Harvard and Yale, both of which were started to train Christians for ministry. The next generation came in and talked about God without actually experiencing Him. Now those institutions are thoroughly secular. Chair 2 people know how to get from earth to heaven, but they don't know how to bring heaven to earth. The next generation does not get to see who the Father really is; they don't know how to disciple a nation.

CARRY THE ATMOSPHERE OF HEAVEN

How do you disciple a nation? You engage with the "seven mountains" of culture - education systems, governments, media, arts and entertainment, families, the business world, and religious institutions - with a kingdom mindset, not to try to dominate them or move them from a Chair 2 mindset by human effort, but to influence them, to bless and not to curse, to carry the atmosphere of heaven into the experiences of the world. You begin to deal with systemic poverty because you understand heaven's economy. You live out kingdom ethics and share kingdom insights. The sons and daughters of glory leave their Chair 1 church to go into the world on Monday morning to pastor, teach, prophesy, and exercise their gifts in their assignment in the marketplace. From a Chair 1 perspective, you will recognize the next Joseph or Esther or Daniel in normal or even unlikely people because you will treat people based upon their destiny, not their history. You will be able to see the apostle Paul when you are looking at the terrorist Saul. You will change the environment around you and raise up a generation of people who influence the world rather than being influenced by it.

THE GREAT HARVEST

I believe God is saying, "I don't want a billion orphans. I want a billion sons and daughters. I want a family."

Many have prophesied the coming of a billion-soul harvest. In 1975, Bob Jones had an experience of dying and seeing heaven. He heard the Lord tell him about this wave of a billion souls coming into the kingdom family. Though many people have come to the Lord since then, we haven't yet seen a distinct move in which a billion souls have said yes to Jesus. Why not? He is preparing the environment of His kingdom on earth not just to receive souls, but to welcome sons and daughters who fit into a family and can understand what it means to be family members. Many in the church have been busy looking for the fire, but God is looking for fireplaces. If we build the fireplaces, He will provide the fire.

I grew up in Norway in the 1970s, and many believers there, as in many other countries at that time, did not think we would be around much longer. A movie called *The Thief in the Night* had recently come out, and I remember how many of us lived in crippling fear, trying to position ourselves for the rapture so we would not have to go through the tribulation. The Soviet Union was threatening to come into Norway, and we were sure the end was near. Jesus was going to come back soon, and we needed to prepare ourselves. We trained ourselves for the rapture—some even had "rapture drills"—and talked about those who would be left behind. Who could possibly dream or envision in that environment? And since we were on our way to heaven, we didn't concern ourselves with much responsibility on earth. Why worry about leaving a legacy for our grandchildren when none of us were going to be here anyway? That is Chair 2 thinking, and it cost us an entire generation and a whole culture. Only 20 percent of the Generation Y, or millennials, think church attendance is important; far fewer consider themselves Bible-based believers.[2] Some of our young people qualify as an unreached people group. They often don't even understand the language we are speaking when we talk about our Father.

---

2 The Barna Group, 2014. http://www.barna.com/research/americans-divided-on-the-importance-of-church/#.V-hxhLVy6FD, accessed March 17, 2017.

The world is watching, and most of what they see in Christians comes from a Chair 2 worldview. I believe up to 90 percent of believers are actually living their lives in Chair 2 on a daily basis. Many visit Chair 1 from time to time, but they create whole theologies, philosophies, businesses, organizations, and approaches to life from a Chair 2 mindset and call it normal Christian life. This is why there is often little visible difference between the church and the world. Take the temperature of Chair 2 and Chair 3, and it is often the same.

We can see the Chair 1 paradigm throughout Jesus' ministry, even in His very identity. When He came up out of the water at His baptism, the Dove descended on Him and the Father said, "This is My beloved Son, in whom I am well pleased" (Matthew 3:17). That's His identity, and it came before any miracles, healings, deliverances, preaching, and teaching. He already had an A+ from His Father. That was the starting point. He experienced the Father's pleasure. Then what happened? He went into the wilderness where He was tempted, and the first words out of the tempter's mouth were, "*If* you are the Son of God . . ." (Matthew 4:3). His identity was questioned. *Did God really say . . .?* The same strategy used against Eve in the garden was used against Jesus. But unlike Adam and Eve, Jesus did not invert the order of being, having, and then doing. He maintained His rest in His identity. You can know your identity, experience His intimacy, receive His inheritance, and walk out your destiny. You can reign in life with Him. This is your privilege as a son or daughter of God. In the following pages we will explore how to make it your everyday experience. Life in the resting place of God—and as a resting place *for* God—changes everything.

PART ONE
IDENTITY

Who Am I?

If you don't have the right sense of identity, in keeping with the Father's perception of you, everything else will be skewed.

The kingdom is a family business made up of Papa God, Jesus, the Holy Spirit, and you as a fourth member of the family. You have a seat right next to Jesus, your older brother. When you know your place in the family, you also know you did nothing to earn it. It's yours. You can rest there.

This place of rest is where everything starts. It was given to you even before the foundation of the world. Ephesians 1:4-5 says we were predestined in love, chosen in Him and adopted by Him before the world was made. Who was I, Leif, before the world was made? Who were you? We may not have occurred on the timeline of history yet, but our identity was already formed in the mind of the Father. We were already connected with Him. Before any other role you live out in this world, you are first and foremost a son or daughter[1] of a good, good Father who loves you intensely. Just having the knowledge of this truth will not help you. It is vital to *agree with Him* about who you are as a chosen and beloved one so that this truth can fill your spirit, your heart, and your mind. You need a revelation of the Father's love, a baptism that immerses you in His love in such a way that you can never forget it. God is a good father who has chosen to delegate the responsibility of this world to a family of sons and daughters. In order to know our true identity, we have to be able to see who God is. We can know who we are when we see Him as He is. Until you see yourself as

---

1 We will talk a lot about sonship, and of course this includes daughters as well. Scripture uses terms like this inclusively: men as part of the "bride of Christ," women as "sons" of God. Rather than specifying each gender in every reference, we will assume members of each gender know they are recipients of all the promises of God.

God sees you, think about yourself the way He thinks about you, and feel the way He feels toward you, you cannot know Him intimately, experience your inheritance, or fulfill your destiny.

LIVING FROM HEAVEN TO EARTH

When you know who you are, whose you are, where you are, and what you have, you can live from heaven to earth rather than from earth toward heaven.

Having the proper identity and the proper family relationships leads to a supernatural lifestyle of inheritance and destiny. It begins with identity. This is the difference between true Christianity and churchianity or religion—between the kingdom and the world, or church as the body of Christ versus church as an orphanage longing for a Father figure. As we will see, when a church becomes like an orphanage and you live from an orphan spirit, two manifestations are possible: you become religious or rebellious, legalistic or lawless, self-righteous or struggle with sin. In none of these instances do you have an influence on the world; rather, you are being influenced by it.

So let's begin this journey to the place of resting and reigning by focusing on identity, the foundation for everything else.

CHAPTER ONE
Reigning from Identity

There is a huge difference between the way a son or daughter sees and the way an orphan sees - sons and daughters see promises, orphans see problems. It is not possible to reveal the Father's heart with an orphan mindset. The true nature of the Father can only be revealed in a kingdom family context. Only the family can love the way the Father loves. Only sons and daughters can produce sons and daughters.

In this restless world that is so disconnected from the Father's heart, there are more than hundreds of thousands (possibly even millions) of orphanages we call churches. This is why the world is longing for the sons and daughters of God to be revealed (Romans 8:19). Many of God's children continue to live with an orphan mentality, unable to display the Father's heart. Only the kingdom family can reproduce churches that see the world as the Father sees it and love as He loves. In fact, that's what the Kingdom Family Movement is all about—loving as the Father loves, becoming a revelation of His heart, and drawing others into the family. *We only have authority over what we love, so loving as the Father loves puts us in a position of being able to exercise authority.* This is why it is so vital to see as the Father sees. Only then can we help a restless world find a place of rest.

A few years ago, I was in a country in Asia and woke up early in the morning to the sounds of a *muezzin* calling the neighborhood to prayer. I couldn't go back to sleep. I turned on the TV, and at that time of the morning, every channel has a Muslim teacher on it. I recognized one of them; I had seen him on TV many times over the years.

"Do you see that person?" the Holy Spirit asked. "I want you to meet him."

This person was very influential; the entire nation could see him teach every morning. But I was very tired and didn't want to meet him. I didn't feel like adding anything to my schedule. Still, the Holy Spirit wouldn't let me let it go.

I contacted my coordinator and asked him to go to this man's headquarters and explain that I wanted to meet him. He tried, and news came back that this would be impossible. We couldn't even get to his secretary's secretary. It wasn't going to work. *I'm off the hook,* I thought!

Then the Holy Spirit said, "No, I didn't ask you to *try* to meet him. I said I wanted you to meet him."

"I don't know how to do that," I said.

"Good."

"It's impossible."

"Even better, Leif. Now we can begin." After a few moments, I heard the voice again. "Leif, when you look at his face, what do you see?"

I knew what my natural eyes saw, but the Holy Spirit didn't ask the question because He lacked an answer. He just wanted me to see what the Father was seeing and think the way He thinks. God knew this man before the foundation of the world. He rejoiced the moment he was born. So who was this person in the Father's heart?

As I listened and waited, the Holy Spirit came clearly to me with a voice that said, "He is a man of peace." That was not yet clear to me in the natural; that's just what the Father was seeing in him. When you get to know the Father's heart, you realize that He sees everyone according to their destiny rather than their past. When Stephen was martyred, most people saw a Saul overseeing the event. God saw a Paul. God saw something in this Muslim teacher too.

I knew this was an invitation to something God wanted to do. I talked with a couple of men who were with me on this trip and told them we were going to this man's headquarters.

"They told you he wouldn't see you," they said. "What's your strategy?"

"I am giving him the peace award of the year," was my reply.

I bought a big glass sculpture and with it we created Global Mission Awareness' first annual Peace Award, and went to this man's headquarters.

"I'm here from the Peace Committee to present him the award

of the year," I told them. They were very curious. Before long, I was in a back room with this leader and gave him my book *Seeing Through Heaven's Eyes*. He gave me one of his books too. Eventually we went into a room where about 100 imams with long beards and dark eyes were staring at me. In one section was a group of women in burkas. I presented the award and honored this man for being a peacemaker. It wasn't false; this was his future identity that he hadn't yet stepped into. Now everyone was beginning to see him this way, as the Father sees him. He looked at himself differently too. By the time the meeting was over, this man took my hand in his, and a long line of imams formed so others could shake my hand. They expressed themselves in ways that were not culturally normal. They realized they were loved. The atmosphere had changed because perfect love casts out fear.

Later, when this man was at a meeting in Washington, D.C., that I attended, he said he wanted to come to my office in Atlanta. We spent three days together. At one point, the presence of God came into my office and got very heavy. I didn't know what to do.

"What is happening here?" this man asked. He was having an experience with the presence of Jesus that was hard to explain.

"What do you mean?" I said.

"I feel these waves, like a tingling going up and down."

At this point, I had enough favor with this man after three years of relationship to ask if I could pray for him. I couldn't touch him, but I felt comfortable enough to put my hand over his head. In the name of Jesus, I released more.

"What's happening?" he said. "It's like fire." He put his hand on his stomach. What I didn't know was that this man had a gluten allergy, and there were certain foods he couldn't eat. The next morning, he went to the breakfast buffet in his hotel and ate everything, even foods that normally would have made him sick. He was healed.

He asked if I could come to his room later and pray for his family members on Skype. I released the presence of God on the computer, and a room in the Middle East was filled with it. I had planned to take him to the airport the next morning for his speaking engagements in California, but he insisted on sitting in my office one last time to get more of what he had experienced. He asked me to pray again, and the glory came in. We could hardly stand. It was an amazing encounter.

I got a call from some imams in San Diego a while later. "What has happened to our leader?" they asked.

"What are you talking about?"

"He says he was with you and something has happened to him. What's going on?" His colleagues in San Francisco and Sacramento noticed the same thing. The environment on this man had changed. When he got back to his country, he noticed beggars and sick people he had never noticed before. He had sympathy for barren women and people who were suffering. What was once just a fact of life was now heavy on his heart.

I got an urgent text from this leader while I was in the Philippines, so I called him. He told me, "I put an ad in the paper telling people to come to the mosque for prayer in Jesus' name. Many imams are here, and I don't know what to do. I told them it would be healing prayer like you did for me, but I don't know how to do that." So I prayed a prayer over the phone. I just gave him clear instructions to close his eyes, rest, and speak in the name of Jesus, and release a healing prayer. As he did, he had an encounter in that moment: when he closed his eyes, he saw me and then saw a picture of Jesus standing behind me. Jesus was very big, and he could clearly see holes in Jesus' hands. As he prayed, many people got healed.

I've been on this journey of learning how to host the presence of God, and I share this story to show what it can look like and what it can lead to. You don't have to be a thermometer that measures the temperature in the room; you can be a thermostat that changes it. You can go underneath the radar to change a culture in a home, a company, a school, an office, an agency, or anywhere. As a son or daughter who has spent time in the Father's presence, you bring His presence into the lives of people around you.

SEEING THE WAY GOD SEES

As I explored in my book *Seeing Through Heaven's Eyes,* there is a war going on for our worldview, and it's much more personal than the culture wars many people are fighting along political or social lines. This war is about the glasses you are wearing. How do you see God? Yourself? The world? The future? What glasses are you wearing? Are they the lenses of the world or the lenses of heaven? Are they focused on self or on Jesus? Are they sunglasses that protect you from the light or Son-glasses that will help you see it?

Multitudes of people, Christian or not, need brand new glasses. *That's what much of this book will be about—seeing the way God sees.* If you are able to get this, it will radically change how you live, empower you supernaturally, and fill your life with the fruitfulness and purpose that you have been longing for. It will bring you into the resting place and also make you a resting place for God. There are four primary areas we will focus on with these new glasses.

THE HARD WORK OF ENTERING INTO REST

We are living in a season when the gospel, the good news of the kingdom, will be preached as a witness and testimony to all nations. The knowledge of the glory of God is going to cover the earth as the water covers the sea (Habakkuk 2:14). The kingdoms of this world are going to become the kingdom of the Lord—through those who know who they are, whose they are, and what they have in Him. Everything God has is made available to you in order for you to fulfill your destiny.

In order to see these four areas of life correctly, as God sees them, we have to have the right glasses on. This is the key to living from our inheritance and fulfilling our destiny, which explains why there is such an intense war going on for our worldview. In the spirit realm, there have already been two world wars. We can see one in the garden back at the beginning of our world, and the other at the cross. But World War III is an ongoing war on worldview for how we see God, how we perceive that He sees us, and how we see the future. In this war, this "hard work" of entering into rest, we have to get the right identity, experience intimacy, know our inheritance, and then walk in our destiny. Every major battle we face in our lives in one way or another will be fought in these areas. The first thing to understand is that the order of these areas is important.

REALIZING WHAT YOU HAVE RECEIVED

I know many believers who are running after their inheritance and destiny before entering into the rest of their identity and intimacy with God. They are striving to achieve rather than realizing what they have received. We will see how this is a distortion of what we were given in Eden, and how it is foundational in this battle for worldview. Most of the world believes they have to *do* something in order to *have* something so they can *be* something. That is not how we were originally designed. In God's design, we *are* something, so we *have* everything, and then can *do* anything. To be specific, we are in a covenant relationship with the Father because we are sons and daughters, and because we are sons and daughters, we have an inheritance, and with that inheritance we can fulfill our assignment, our destiny. *Being*, then *having*, then *doing*. You will find that your natural tendency as a result of the fall is to do in order to have, and to have in order to be. That is why most people in the world are trying to find their identity in what they do and what they have and are always falling short. They never get to the place of true identity. They don't know how to be sons and daughters of the Father. They invert the order by doing, then having, then being.

RENEWING YOUR MIND

It all begins with identity—seeing ourselves as God sees us, thinking and feeling about ourselves as He does, and loving ourselves as He does because we can never love Him or others until we've experienced His love ourselves. Then we grow in intimacy with Him. We become what we behold, and whatever we become we are then able to release. The world's system of doing something in order to become something doesn't work. Our minds have a hard time grasping the truth—that we *are* and then we *do*. That's one of the primary reasons we have to step out of conformity with this world and let our minds be renewed (Romans 12:1-2). It's the only way to recognize who we are and whose we are.

REIGNING FROM THE FATHER'S LOVE

I know I am a beloved son. My Papa loves me, adores me, delights in me. I'm His happy thought. He is for me and not against me. This is the starting point, the beginning. Knowing this enables me to experience the presence of the Father in His home and live in a place of peace—*shalom*. We have communion there. We are together, united in a covenant of love and intimacy. I gaze at His face, and then when I look in the mirror I see myself totally differently. I hear His voice from a place of love. *In the resting place, as I commune with a God who loves the world, I begin to love the way He loves, and then I can reign with Him as He reigns.* Fear is gone because perfect love casts out fear (1 John 4:18). Love begins to motivate me to do what I see the Father doing. Only from identity and intimacy do I begin to realize the inheritance I have. Only after I have answered the questions of who I am and where I am can I begin to answer the question, "What do I have?"

There is abundance in the Father's house, more than enough in the family account to have everything I need to do what I have been called to do. Jesus paid for everything on the cross. He inherits everything, and I am a co-heir with Him. His inheritance is my inheritance. With this knowledge, I can begin to grasp my destiny. Yes, the world is dark, but in the middle of the darkness, I am going to rise and shine with the glory that is rising upon me, just as Isaiah 60 says. God is raising up culture changers in this generation who will tip the balance in this war on worldview. Light is penetrating the darkness because we are getting new glasses that change the way we think. Our minds are being renewed. From the resting place—knowing our identity, intimacy, inheritance, and destiny—we reign with Him and begin to change the world.

CHAPTER ONE DEVOTIONAL
Reigning from Identity

God longs for you to know that you are one of His dearly beloved children; that He adores you, delights in you, and loves you so passionately that He gave His Son for you. When you come into the truth of your God-given identity, you can start living as a beloved son or daughter in the Father's house where you will experience intimacy and love. From that secure place in His embrace you will begin to realize your Kingdom inheritance. As you put these aspects of your life together – identity, intimacy and inheritance – in that order, you will find yourself on your way to your destiny, to that place of ruling and reigning from the Father's love.

On the way to your destiny you will acquire Kingdom skills that will change you and in turn change the world around you. You will learn what it means to enter into the hard work of rest, to see the way God sees, to hear His voice, love the way He loves. With a renewed mind, in this place of intimacy, love replaces fear and problems become promises as you reign with Him as He reigns.

FOCUS AREAS

» Authority – Loving as the Father loves puts you in a position of being able to exercise authority. We only have authority over what we love.

» Striving versus Receiving – striving to achieve instead of realizing what you have received – a distortion of Eden

» Renewing your Mind – seeing as God sees, loving as He loves, entering into the overflow of intimacy

REFLECTION QUESTIONS

1. Chapter 1 has introduced you to the concept of an orphan heart versus the heart of a son or daughter of God. Why is it that orphans see problems whereas children of God see promises?

2. The Kingdom Family Movement is about loving as the Father loves, becoming a revelation of His heart, and drawing others into the family. How does being part of God's family reveal His heart to the world?

3. Throughout the book you will find an emphasis on entering into God's rest. Chair 1 is a place of God's rest. You cannot sit in the arms of the Father and be restless. Take a few moments to reflect on your ability to get into the place of rest with God in the midst of daily life. What are some of the things keeping you from a place of rest with your heavenly Father?

CHAPTER TWO
The Blueprint

For most of my life, I had a view of God that was not very healthy and as a result I didn't know who I was. I saw God as angry and authoritative, sometimes very critical and focused on my faults. That isn't the view I have today, of course, and it wasn't even what I would have said theologically about my beliefs. But at a heart level, it was ingrained in me from an early age. I was comfortable with Jesus and even with the Holy Spirit. I would say I knew the Spirit pretty well, in fact. But I didn't know my Papa. I didn't see His heart. I saw Him as a holy God—and He certainly is—but in my mind, His holiness turned Him away from me every time I sinned. Then it was up to me to repent, which meant feeling as sorry as I could for what I had done. My perspective was a lot like that of someone who thinks he has to get cleaned up before he takes a bath. If I could get everything in order in my life, then the Father would be able to turn back toward me. Any sin in my life would hinder my intimacy with Him.

That may seem very spiritual, but it actually leads to a self-centered way of life. Everything was about *me* and how well *I* did. You get very focused on self that way, and your life with God becomes centered on what *you* can and cannot do. You feel as if you have to perform to become a mature son or daughter, not as though you already are one. In other words, you disagree with what God says about you.

I still remember the day that view was transformed, when I experienced a baptism in the Father's love. It was a significant turning point in my life. From that point forward, I began to discover who I really am. That's why this question of "Who am I?" must always begin with our view of God. We only realize who we are by realizing who He is and how He sees us. When I got this new revelation—and it was a process for it to really sink in—I heard the Father say one day, *"Son, do you know that when you sin it is actually you who are turning away from Me, and that I'm still standing there with open arms? I should be the safest place for you, even in your worst moments. When your children fall, don't you want them to feel comfortable enough to come to you for help?"* I realized at that moment that I had missed many opportunities over the years because I had a wrong view of the Father. I had been operating as an orphan rather than a son. I was doing things so I could have something, and hoping to have something so I could become something. This transformation in my thinking led me to a life-changing paradigm shift and into the picture of the three chairs. I realized that we cannot really understand who we are and how we got to where we are without going all the way back to the beginning—to the way we were meant to be.

BEFORE THE BEGINNING

The culture of heaven is our template for love and interdependence.

If I could take you all the way back to eternity past, you would find there a Father, a Son, and a Spirit. They are three but completely one. This God in three persons was there independently of anything that ever existed. When the Bible describes creation, it says, "In the beginning, God . . ." The Word begins with God and ends with God. But when Genesis talks about God in the beginning, it uses the word *elohim*—a plural noun. In the beginning, the Father, Son, and Spirit were a family. They had an amazing, equal relationship with no competition between them. They were and are the prototype of love and honor. If you were to ask which one of them was most important, the Father would point to the Spirit and the Son, the Son would point to the Spirit and the Father, and the Spirit would point to the Father and the Son. They were in a covenant of perfect love with one another—completely united as one.

Why is this pattern important? Because if we don't understand the blueprint of God's family and how He intended things to be in the beginning—that everything in the kingdom family is relational—we will start to create our own blueprints from an unhealthy worldview seated in Chair 2. We will make Him in our own image and then ask Him to bless what we are doing rather than do what He is blessing. Self will be in the center. We will turn the family atmosphere into a matter of principles and productivity. When our template is the culture of heaven, we see what a culture of love and honor looks like and how selfless it is. We see how total agreement can work—what it's like not to compete with one another but to complete or complement one another. This is a blueprint for covenant and the kingdom family and a picture of what God wants to establish on earth.

THE TRUTH DEFICIENCY

A truth deficiency led to a love deficiency, which becomes a blessing deficiency.

In this heavenly environment, among a vast host of angels in heaven was a very prominent angel or archangel named Lucifer—a bright, beautiful morning star who reflected the glory of the Father. He seems to have been a worship leader whose responsibility was to gaze at the Father, Son, and Spirit and be amazed. He was created to appreciate God's "wow" effect, and he had a certain "wow" effect himself. He was dazzling.

God loved Lucifer because God is love. So how did Lucifer fall from heaven and become the deceiver and the adversary? He didn't love himself the way the Father loved him. He did not join in the culture of the Father, Son, and Spirit, who could each point at the others as most valued or most beautiful. He apparently decided that if he became like the Father, Son, and Spirit, he would feel better about himself. His distorted sense of identity intervened (you can read about his fall in Isaiah 14:12-14). It started with a truth deficiency, which led to a love deficiency, which eventually became a blessing deficiency. His root thinking—the truth deficiency—was a desire to be equal to the Most High. "Why are you God and I'm just a worship leader?" We never see this kind of identity crisis with Jesus in the gospels. Never did He ask, "Why am I just a Son while you are the Father?" Jesus was completely secure. The members of the Trinity honor each other equally. But Lucifer had an issue with his identity and was insecure. He wanted to be like God, to sit on the throne. Because he didn't see himself or love himself the way the Father saw and loved him, he left the family. He seemed to think, *If I do something, then I'll have something, and then I can be something.* I, I, I . . . the focus that has led to the world system we live in today.

Because of this root identity issue, Lucifer was not one with the Father. He broke covenant. He violated the family culture. He left in rebellion and took a third of the angels with him. They became fallen angels, an entire army we know from Scripture as demons. They no longer have a home or a father. They have no place of security or affirmation, no experience of perfect love, no sense of value. They are orphans.

THE IDENTITY THIEF

You probably know the story from Genesis 3. The devil, the fallen archangel Lucifer, was very clever. He came with an orphan spirit in the body of a serpent and caused Adam and Eve to question the nature of God. "Did God really say . . .?" Or, to paraphrase, "Is God really good, and are you really good enough?" He told them they would not really die; that God was deceiving them, and if they ate from the forbidden tree, they would actually become like God Himself. In other words, "If you do, you will have, and then you will become." He inverted the order of their identity and inheritance

The Age-Old Lie

» You can become something by doing something.

» You aren't really who God says you are until you strive for it and achieve it.

» You can become something better than what God says you are.

Of course, Eve wanted to be like Papa. It had not occurred to her to do something in order to become something, but it seemed to make sense. She stepped out of agreement with what the Father had said. She broke her unity with Him; they were no longer one. The irony is that the enemy tempted her with something she already had—God's likeness. He suggested that God was withholding something from His son and daughter, even though they had already been made in God's image. How could they become more "like God" than being in His image? The orphan spirit always feels insufficient and thinks that something more must be done. The enemy tempted Eve with an orphan mentality because that's exactly what he had.

As soon as Eve and then Adam heeded the serpent's voice, the world became an orphanage and began seeking identity in things other than God. We believed the lie that there is a higher or better identity than being a son or daughter of the Most High. But there isn't. That is as high as it gets. That's our identity. Everything else is an assignment.

As a result of this broken unity, Adam and Eve were no longer in the garden. They lost sight of who they were and whose they were. Their identity, intimacy, and inheritance became distorted because the enemy is an identity thief. They began living like they didn't have a home or a family, trying to *do* in order to *have* in order to *become*. They and their descendants became very competitive, not operating from a place of rest but from a place of restlessness. But the bully messed with the wrong girl, and God started His restoration plan. He stepped between Eve and the serpent and prophesied Satan's destruction - the seed of the woman would crush the serpent.

RECOGNIZING LUCIFER'S STRATEGY

Most people still live in the culture of the fall, even after they become Christians. "If we only had a better government, if we only had more money, if we only had better education ...," and on and on. Prayers become, "Jesus, please come back because it's getting so dark and difficult here. I don't know if I can handle it anymore." They are rooted in fear rather than love, anxiety rather than hope, restlessness rather than rest. They are still buying into the lie that if we eat of the tree we can become like God—we can *do*, then *have*, then *become*. This is still Lucifer's strategy—to keep us from operating within family as sons and daughters.

Every sickness and disease, all evil and oppression and division, are rooted in Lucifer's nature after his fall. He is influencing entire armies of angels that want to keep you from Chair 1 where you can hear the Father's voice and be a prophetic voice. He wants us to put fig leaves over our pain and scars—to fear intimacy and vulnerability that will bring us back into union with God. He strategizes to insulate us with guilt, loneliness, escapism, insecurities, or anything else that manifests either in rebellion or religion, causing us pain. Our pain will always seek pleasure because that's what pain does.

If you don't know how much you are loved, you will have hidden, core areas in your soul that love has not touched.

The enemy will find the right buttons to push to make you restless and get you to eat from the wrong tree again and again. His lies are the root of addictions, compulsions, and those deep wounds that keep us seeking after inner healing. The religious response to this restlessness is to fill the void in our hearts with activity. We go out in the field to work for God because the more we do for Him, the more valuable we feel. It's good to go to Bible studies, prayer meetings, and soaking sessions to cultivate intimacy with the Father, but it's also a very subtle temptation to do these things in order to become someone valuable. That's still the same lie. I did it for a long time in ministry. You can have 15,000 in a meeting, then 20,000, then 50,000—and it will never be enough. Whatever we accomplish cannot ever validate us as sons or daughters. We keep craving more because we're never filled until we get into the resting place where we see, hear, feel, and experience the Father and receive His blessing just for being—just like in Eden.

We see these distortions everywhere in the world today. It's why people blame each other for problems and compete with each other for honors. This is why we have problems with elections, why Sunnis and Shiites fight each other, why jealousy keeps us from honoring one another, and on and on. We cover up our false identity and false intimacy with fig leaves because we no longer see His face, hear His voice, feel His love, experience His presence, and abide in His pleasure. Instead of His pleasure we feel pressure because the entire world system shifted from *being* to *doing*. Everyone wants to *do* and *have* in order to *be*.

EDEN'S DESIGN

Eden - the perfect place – with God – with a perfect destiny.

When God decided to create a place called earth, cultivate a garden named Eden, and put human beings within it, He said, "Let Us make man in Our image, according to Our likeness" (Genesis 1:27). Did you notice that He said, "Let **us** . . ."? Because He wanted to create what He had in heaven—a holy family, a prototype of fellowship that loves like the Father, Son, and Spirit love, honors the way they

63

honor, celebrates uniqueness but also unity. He created Adam and Eve to be distinct, told them to be fruitful and multiply and fill the earth, and then offered them the possibility of establishing dominion over the earth. The Father, Son, and Spirit wanted the fellowship and environment of heaven to fill the earth.

God created man first - on the sixth day of creation, God shaped dust into a prototype of His image and breathed into this form's nostrils. What was lifeless was suddenly filled with life. The very first thing Adam saw was the face of a loving Father. I believe the first thing he said was a gasp of "Ab"—the Hebrew word for father. God breathed into him, and Adam drew that first breath in with *Ab* and exhaled with *ba*: Ab-ba—a sound of delight and enthusiasm when a child sees his Father. The first feeling he felt was perfect love. The first voice he heard was the sound of a loving Father. The first experience he had was the presence of the Father. His first home was a place of pleasure—a Hebrew meaning of "Eden." The only thing he knew was a relationship. He was soon introduced to the family mission—a covenant and a kingdom assignment. So Adam's original design and condition was to be in the image of God, in the presence and love of God, in face-to-face gaze with God, full of God's breath, and living in a place of God's pleasure.

Why is this significant? Because it tells us about God's desire for us and describes what our Chair 1 position is to be like. The first full day of Adam's existence was the seventh day of God's creation—a day of rest. Adam began his existence not in a place of doing or having but simply in a place of being. He began in a resting place.

Then God put Adam to sleep. It's amazing what happens when we find a place of rest. God can do something through us; He can reproduce something. While Adam was asleep, God took one of his ribs, and even though everything God had made was good—and Adam was "very good"—what God did next was perhaps the pinnacle of creation. He created Eve because it was not good for Adam to be alone. God wanted a family, a reflection of the fellowship of heaven. The Bible says God *brought* Eve to Adam (Genesis 2:22), which means she had some time alone with the Father before she was united with Adam. She, too, saw the face of her Father, heard His voice, felt His love, captured the fullness of His presence and His gaze, and experienced His pleasure, just as Adam did. She didn't need anything; she was already complete, made in God's image, and at rest in the resting place. God brought Eve to Adam for them to come into a covenant relationship of love.

This was before the fall and before the curse. Adam and Eve were in the perfect place with a perfect God with a perfect destiny in front of them. This son and daughter of the Father were given an assignment together, not to compete with each other but to complete each other. Neither was more important—any conflict or competition came later as a result of the curse. In Chairs 2 and 3 today, we see women being oppressed and their identity devalued. That's the fallen world system. But in Chair 1, women are being lifted up because that has always been the heart of the Father. Adam and Eve were two but one, just as the Father, Son, and Spirit are three but one.

Eden's Blueprint

» The way God's kingdom works is that what you have received, you can be; what you have become, you can multiply; and what you multiply, you can have dominion over.

» You have authority over what you become and over what you love.

» Because you receive, you become, and because you become, you can multiply and have authority. That was the blueprint from the beginning.

GOD'S GLORY

In the perfect environment of the Garden, God blessed them, both male and female (Genesis 1:28). The world is full of people today who have never experienced the Father's blessing. They don't know their identity because they have not heard Him declare it over them. They don't know who they really are, who they were designed to be, or the family they were born into. They are not seeing His face, hearing His voice, sensing His love, experiencing His presence, and living in His presence. Each one of us is designed for the same kind of love and intimacy with the Father that Adam and Eve experienced. They are prototypes of who you are, your identity. You are God-made—in His image and declared to be "very good." His likeness is in you. *Your starting point—the starting point for everything, in fact—is God's glory.*

The religious mind does not understand this glory. Religion focuses on the failure of human beings rather than on the faithfulness of God. It highlights sin and how all of us have fallen short of glory. But there is something glorious in each one of us. That's the starting point. Sin made us fall short of the glory we were designed to express and experience, but that's why Jesus came—to restore us back to glory. *We are not human doings; we are human beings!*

It is important to see Eden as a blueprint for our design and as a reflection of how things were in heaven. If we don't, the human tendency is to create a model here on earth—the Tower of Babel is one example, but we each have our own ways—and then try to build toward heaven. That's what religion generally tries to do, but it will never work because it doesn't function from the proper blueprint. It doesn't grasp our foundational identity as sons and daughters of God who already experience His pleasure before ever doing anything good or bad. Adam and Eve had their identity and their blessing as a son and daughter of the Father before they were ever told to do anything. It is more than a matter of semantics that God says, "Be fruitful," rather than "Bear fruit" or "Do fruitful things." Their first assignment was to *be*. They received the blessing of fruitfulness and dominion from their Father by just being. Adam and Eve had not yet earned anything. They had only received.

Now, only after his identity and intimacy with the Father was fully established, was Adam assigned to take care of the garden. There were two trees in the garden—the tree of life and the tree of the knowledge of good and evil. From one tree, there would always be fullness and abundance. It was a tree of trust, a tree that demonstrated that Adam and Eve believed their Father and received His blessing freely. The tree of life bore the fruits of love, joy, peace, and everything else that flows from the fellowship of the Father, Son, and Spirit. But God didn't want robots, so He gave them a choice. They would not be forced to love; they had freedom. God told them not to eat from the tree of the knowledge of good and evil. If they ate from that tree, they would no longer be able to see His face, hear His voice, experience His presence, feel His love, and enjoy the intimacy that comes from identity as a son or daughter. Something in them would die.

ALIGNMENT LEADS TO ASSIGNMENT

We look up, what is up comes into us, what is in us comes out of us, and what comes out moves us forward.

All of us have been affected by the fall. We were designed for Chair 1, but Chairs 2 and 3 have become "normal life" for most of the world. Chair 2 Christians may learn some Chair 1 principles and visit from time to time, but few of us live there. When we are in Kingdom alignment we are able to see God's face, hear His voice, feel His love, experience His presence, and live in His pleasure. When all of these things are in place and we are aligned, we attract the Father's blessing, which unlocks our destiny. Our alignment leads us into our assignment.

Until we come into Chair 1, we don't realize that the things we see around us become part of our assignment. We have to come into agreement and become one with Father God and with one another and then join in this mission to get His family back. Creation began with a family and ends with a family—from Father, Son, and Spirit to a family from every nation, tribe, and tongue (Revelation 7:9). It started well and will end well. *The enemy is constantly trying to keep believers in Chair 2 because he knows that in Chair 1 we can see the Father's face, hear His voice, feel His love, experience His presence, and live in His pleasure.* That changes the way we see God—in His presence, you recognize that He is full of love and goodness—and it changes the way you see others. You are filled with His love, joy, and peace because you become what you behold, and then you carry these blessings into the world and draw people back to the Father.

The curse of the orphan spirit will be broken when the fatherless spirit is undone and hearts are restored back to their Father in the identity and intimacy of the resting place.

Before the fall, the Father provided everything. There was no gray hair, no pimples, no threats to survival, nothing. The world was a perfect place with a perfect God. But when the curse came in, sin began to grow like a cancer. God was not finished, of course. He established a covenant with Abraham and gave him a blessing and a promise for his seed. He made a covenant with Moses, promising to deliver His people from slavery into a promised land. He made a covenant with David, promising to establish his throne forever. We see all kinds of God-given covenants in this orphan world—small pictures pointing toward something greater to come. The Old Testament ends with the word "curse" (Malachi 4:6). It comes in a promise to turn the hearts of fathers toward their children and children toward their fathers. It addresses the curse of an orphaned world.

After 400 years between the testaments, we see covenants beginning to be fulfilled. The genealogies of Matthew and Luke tie the birth of Jesus to ancient promises. The son of Abraham is Isaac—a picture of the lamb. The son of David is Solomon—*shalom*, or peace. Jesus is the perfect image of God who came to restore us to our original likeness. He is the Son of God who came to restore us to our original identity. God had a plan from the beginning because He's a covenant-keeping God. Jesus was slain before the foundation of the world (Revelation 13:8), which means God had a plan even before the fall. He had already made provision. He was restoring our identity and intimacy so we could receive our inheritance and fulfill our destiny. *God wanted His family back, and He still does.*

CHAPTER TWO DEVOTIONAL
The Blueprint

God has a design for His family. Adam and Eve's original design and condition was to be in the image of God, in the presence and love of God, to live in face-to-face gaze with God, full of His breath, and living in a place of His pleasure. This is a picture of what life looks like in Chair 1. There is fellowship, relationship and stewardship that allows us to complete, not compete. In this kind of a relationship with God, you receive from Him, which enables you to become who He created you to be. From the place of identity, you can multiply and have authority. It all begins in the presence of God's glory. Your alignment with God leads to your assignment in this life. Problems will become promises as you see the world through God's eyes.

FOCUS AREAS

» The Identity Thief – the age-old lie that began in the Garden.

» The Truth Deficiency – identity confusion violates the Kingdom family culture and leads to an orphan spirit.

» Recognizing Lucifer's Strategy – to keep us from intimacy with God.

REFLECTION QUESTIONS

1. How would you explain the concept that our starting point for a relationship with God begins with an understanding of His glory?

2. How does a religious mindset differ from Kingdom family mindset?

3. How would you describe your inheritance from God?

4. What is your understanding of the statement "You only have authority over what you become and what you love"?

REFLECTION

Take time to reflect on the culture of heaven as it is illustrated in the perfect covenant relationship between the Trinity – the forever love union between Father, Son and Holy Spirit that Jesus brought to earth for us to embrace – allowing it to draw you into the place of a beloved son or daughter of the Father.

CHAPTER THREE

Baptism of Love

I spent years in Chair 2 before I experienced a baptism of the Father's love that changed my life. His love went to the deepest roots of fear in my life that caused me to live from an orphan spirit. His perfect love cast out fear and made me feel His pleasure, not pressure. I felt His liquid love going into me, and it touched the deepest root fear in my life. As His perfect love went in, I was delivered and cleansed. I heard an audible voice that said, *"Leif, you are Mine. You are My beloved. I love you. I like you. I delight in you. You don't have to do anything. We will do much together, but I don't value you for what you do. I just want you for you. Come home."*

When I came out of the encounter, I wept for several hours and expressed myself in ways Norwegians normally don't do! I had been stoic before; now I was a son. My Father loves me! He likes me! Something shifted. Many doors of opportunity opened before me that had never opened before. When I was in Chair 2, I needed opportunity in order to feel valuable and significant or to get my needs met. But once I knew I was a son, I didn't need anything! The whole world began to open up.

In simple theology, Jesus took my F and gave me an A+. He took my report card and gave me His. What is true of Him is now true of me. When I woke up to that grace, it was overwhelming. He did not treat me according to my mess and give me what I deserved. He treated me as a son in whom He was well pleased. Then He said, "This is the way I want you to treat the world. I have forgiven you; forgive them. As I've loved you, go and love them." He sent me out to change the environment in the same way the environment inside me had been changed.

OPERATING FROM THE DEPTHS OF HIS LOVE

When I am in Chair 1, I am focused on the Father. I am overwhelmed with His goodness and kindness. I can see His face, hear His voice, sense His presence, and feel His love. It is a place of rest. I am energized and empowered by the Dove. When I am squeezed, love comes out. My desire is to bring heaven to earth and see the Father's kingdom come where I am.

When I am in Chair 2, I experience restlessness. I don't see His face or hear His voice very well. I may know about His love, but I don't really feel it. I am trying to live off of my own energy and power and end up drained and fatigued. Instead of the Dove, I have pigeon religion! When I get squeezed, something other than love comes out—anger, frustration, bitterness, or something else that doesn't feel very good. Rather than bringing heaven to earth, my focus is only on getting myself and others to heaven, without any confidence that He is doing something amazing in the here and now.

If you find yourself in unrest, unable to be at peace and constantly striving toward who you think God wants you to be, you are in Chair 2, and that's where the enemy wants to keep you. He would have preferred to keep you in darkness in Chair 3, but having lost that battle, his next best strategy is to keep you in Chair 2, where you can know about your Father but not really know the depths of His love. In that place, you will continue to be restless, striving to perform and become, but wearing yourself out.

The differences between Chairs 1 and 2 are dramatic:

» In Chair 2, you are a thermometer that measures the temperature; in Chair 1, you are a thermostat that sets it.

» In Chair 2, you treat people according to their history; in Chair 1, you treat them according to their destiny.

» In Chair 2, you are annoying; in Chair 1, you are anointed.

» In Chair 2, you say, "Come, Jesus, come." In Chair 1, you hear the Father saying, "Go, church, go—because I'm not coming until you're going."

SEEING FROM HEAVEN'S VIEW

We often do not realize which lenses we are using to look at the world. Our view seems natural to us. We aren't used to seeing from heaven's view.

» Chair 2 people are always talking about how big the problems are, while Chair 1 people are always talking about how big God is.

» Chair 2 thinks we have a darkness problem in the world. Chair 1 recognizes that it's only a lack of light and that there's something we can do about it because we know how to shine.

» Chair 2 sees all the giants in the Chair 3 world, but Chair 1 is busy raising up giant-slayers. [1]

» Those in Chair 2 are overwhelmed by circumstances; those in Chair 1 are overwhelmed by the Father's goodness, kindness, love, beauty, and splendor.

Chair 1 thinking actually results in dancing with joy. It's contagious. You know Jesus not only for who He is to you but who He is *through* you. When you get a revelation of who He is, like Peter did in Matthew 16:16 when he declared Jesus to be the Christ, you also get a revelation of who you are. Like Peter, God wants to use you to build His church. You can begin to live from the identity of that revelation. You can become kingdom possessed and start an epidemic where Jesus rules and reigns in every area of life!

1 My book *Giant Slayers* explores how to walk in a Chair 1 lifestyle of victory and overcoming.

I was recently sharing about this in a Latin American country, and one ministry leader suddenly got new glasses—I call them Son-glasses because they enable us to see as a son and to see as the Son sees. With tears in his eyes, he confessed that he had been leading an entire movement from Chair 2, focused on the problems of his country and not the promises of God. He and his colleagues were focused on the darkness surrounding them rather than on the light available to them. Their diagnosis of the country was right, but it wasn't the whole truth. It wasn't the view from heaven. When his vision changed, he looked at his government and his society no longer with judgment but with hope. He experienced an amazing transformation.

Today we are seeing changed lives, families, churches, and companies. Entire industries are being transformed in different parts of the world. We are experimenting with kingdom truths, and they are working. Government health systems are broken, but kingdom health care works! Kingdom economics are breaking systemic poverty because sons and daughters of God are blessed to be a blessing. This paradigm creates a church that loves the world because we see it as God sees it, and love as God loves. When self is not in the center, everyone benefits (including self). The gifts of the kingdom do not need to be achieved; they are simply received. Everything is a gift.

DREAMING WITH GOD

I once read in *Time* magazine about a region of the world that produced 80 percent of the suicide bombers. No missionary or even any believers had ever been there—2,000 years of Chair 3 darkness, where Satan had cornered a million and a half people who had never heard about the light. I felt that this was an invitation to dream with God. I went into that region for five years with a Chair 2 paradigm as if it were a problem to be solved, but then Psalm 2:7-8 began to become very clear. Verse 7 is a declaration from the Father to the Son based on a relationship: "The Lord has said to Me, 'You are My Son, today I have begotten You.'" The next verse comes in that context, with that relationship having been established: "'Ask of Me, and I will give You the nations for Your inheritance, and the ends of the earth for Your possession'." That's a Kingdom family prayer from a Chair 1 perspective, focused on the opportunity and not the problem. This became the first nation I asked for, not as a problem to solve but as a gift to be received. As I was landing in one of this nation's cities, I said, "Papa, I just want to ask you to receive this beautiful nation."

When we are able to see a circumstance with the lenses of Son-glasses, we are not pleading for what we don't have. Connected with the Father and the Son, we listen to the Holy Spirit and unwrap the gift that is right in front of us. A Chair 2 prayer might ask, "Father, I ask You to give me the nation," but it's from an orphan perspective, a place of desperation and need rather than from a place of promise and expectation. But when I come into Chair 1 as a beloved son, I pray from a different spirit. I pray with the awareness that everything—

every meeting, every situation, every conversation—has to come from Him, go through Him, and go back to Him. "Papa, I know a nation in darkness is not a problem to be achieved but a promise to be received. I don't know how to do it, but I want to receive it from You. There's only darkness there, and You have so much light. It's full of fear, but You have so much love. You are the promise and the answer. I'm asking You to receive it." That prayer eventually led to the breakthrough for the ministry leader in Latin America that I mentioned previously. When we are able to live from the resting place and reign with God there, He does incredible things.

SONS AND DAUGHTERS SIT IN CHAIR 1

I used to give my life to traditional evangelism and church planting, believing that if we planted more churches and got more people saved, the world would get better. That's what I was taught. But it was a lie; the world was still a mess. It's possible to have thousands of churches and still have widespread poverty in the same region. That's evident in many places in Africa and other parts of the world. It's possible to have churches everywhere and still have a 50 percent divorce rate. American society is a testament to this.

There is a difference between having Christians everywhere and having sons and daughters who know how to bring heaven to earth everywhere.

The difference between Christians and sons and daughters is between Chair 1 and Chair 2. Even when both are Christians, they are unequally yoked if they sit in different chairs. The differences are that significant.

A Chair 2 lifestyle can be exhausting. If your value is based on what you do, you will always be doing because what you do will never be enough. The Father is inviting you into a resting place, where you will be empowered to soar like an eagle, roar like a lion, and love like a lamb. You don't need to achieve in this place; you can simply receive. You can move through this anxious, restless world without any restlessness at all.

I heard a story about a young girl who was on an airplane when it went through some extreme turbulence. The plane felt like a rollercoaster, going up and down and side to side, unsettling all the passengers. But while many of the passengers were screaming out in fear and discomfort, the girl remained calm and kept smiling. She was in Chair 1. Finally, the flight began to settle back down to normal, and one of the adults sitting near her who had been fascinated by her reaction decided to ask her about it. "Why weren't you afraid?"

"Oh, my father is the captain," she said. "He can take us through any storm."

The girl knew her father and had complete confidence in him, so there was no need to be worried or restless. She was in a "resting place" because of her relationship with her father.

That's what God is going to do for us in this season, no matter how much shaking is going on. He has not given us a spirit of fear. We know the captain of the plane. He will take us through the storms as a victorious group of people. He will show us who we really are as anointed sons and daughters of a good Father. He will show us how to have Chair 1 marriages, families, businesses, schools, and churches. He will position us as influencers who can bring transformation and offer rest for a world in desperate need of shalom. *The world is looking for a God that looks just like Jesus. They will find Him through believers who have found their identity in Him.*

COMING INTO AGREEMENT WITH HEAVEN

Years ago, I was doing an event with Bill Johnson and Randy Clark in Southampton, England. I had heard a couple of powerful testimonies from my spiritual sons and daughters about how Bill's assistant, Judy Franklin, had helped people have face-to-face encounters with God. I asked Bill if it was okay for Judy to pray for me since she has such grace in this area. As Judy began to pray, I let my sanctified imagination loose and began going on a journey. In the next moment, I was walking along a path with a waterfall behind me, trees on one side, and a big wall. I came to a big wooden door with a handle with a circle, and there was lock with a big O in it. I had to take the circle and open the lock. I walked in and found myself in a different place that led to a park bench. Jesus came and sat with me. I couldn't see His face, but I knew who He was. I could see a light as I tried to look at Him. Questions began to come up in my mind. *"Why didn't I get healed when I had prayed for healing?"* and all sorts of questions like that came flooding into my thoughts. I was trying to stop them, but finally one came out of my mouth. *"Jesus, do I really love You?"* That was not a question I had been thinking about. I knew He loved me, but I didn't really know if I loved Him. He didn't answer. He just patted me on my back with a smile, almost as if He was about to laugh. I could feel it. In the next moment, I was back in the room in Southampton, weeping and totally undone.

Judy looked at me and began to describe the details of my experience, and I knew then that this journey had been more than just sanctified imagination. "How did you know?" I asked her.

"I was up there with you," she said. "I saw it."

This was strange for someone like me, with so much evangelical background in me. This was not normal.

"Now in the next five years," Judy continued, "you will see the evidence of this. You will be known all over the world as an ambassador of love."

That was interesting, and I thought it was a good word. The conference continued, and I spoke that Saturday. A month and half later, I was in a Muslim country. I met one of the top imams in that country. He had a long beard and stared at me; it did not feel like a very seeker-friendly atmosphere. Out of nowhere, he walked up to me and said, "You are the ambassador of love." I was shocked. This kind of expression was not even in their normal language or culture. It's not something a Muslim would say.

From that point, I began to come into agreement with what heaven was seeing for me. This imam was the first one to confirm what Judy had prayed, but it continued. When he looked at me and made that statement, something hit me; I began to change how I saw myself. From then on, in about a dozen different places, the same thing happened. What was a private statement spoken to me from the Father became a public identity. I've even seen people struggle to find words before coming up with "ambassador of love" or "ambassador of peace" in different settings. But it only happened as I came into an agreement with what the Father had already seen in me. As I started to see it, people started to say it. It started to spread, and today I am known in many countries as an ambassador of love.

We were born for face-to-face encounters and intimate conversations with God. He wants us to fully experience His love, attention, and pleasure, to see or sense His facial expressions as He adores us and interacts with us. We were created to experience His fullness by knowing the height, depth, length, and width of His love. This encounter was the first of many I've had with the Lord, and they are every believer's birthright as His sons and daughters. We were made for intimacy.

CHAPTER THREE DEVOTIONAL
Baptism of Love

G od has a baptism of love for you – a place close to His heart. From this intimate place you will be able to see the world as God sees it, to feel what His heart feels – to operate from the depths of His love in the midst of every challenging circumstance. The closer you draw to the Father's burning heart of love, the more it will change your inner environment, equipping you to change the environment around you. Instead of constantly being impacted by the world, you will be the one doing the impacting.

FOCUS AREAS

» Operating from the depths of His love – trading pigeon religion for the Dove.

» Seeing through heaven's eyes – chair 2 sees problems, chair 1 sees promises.

» Dreaming with God – God's desires will become your dreams when you operate from His love.

REFLECTION QUESTIONS

1. How would you explain the statement "be a thermostat that sets the temperature instead of a thermometer that takes the temperature"?

2. In what ways does a religious mindset differ from Kingdom family mindset?

3. Explain the difference between treating people according to their history versus treating them according to their God-given destiny.

4. Imagine if you were constantly overwhelmed by the Father's goodness, kindness, love, beauty and splendor rather than by circumstances. How would that change your life?

REFLECTION

Reflect on Psalm 2:8 - "'Ask of Me, and I will give You the nations for Your inheritance, and the ends of the earth for Your possession',", thinking about how it would feel to make this verse part of your prayers.

PART ONE SUMMARY REFLECTION:
IDENTITY

Who Am I?

In chapter 1 we explored the issue of an orphan spirit versus living as a beloved son or daughter of God by highlighting four areas to be examined in depth later – identity, intimacy, inheritance, and destiny. Chapter 2 introduced the concept of God's design for humanity – that we live in a love relationship as He demonstrates it to us through the Trinity. Chapter 3 talks about allowing the love of God to transform our hearts and minds so that we can love the world like He does.

ACTIVATION

»   Make a list of the areas of your thinking that need to give way
    to the love of God for your heart and mind to be transformed.

»   Go back through chapters 1, 2 and 3, highlighting those places
    in need of focus in your life.

»   Reflect on where you are in your understanding of each of the
    four areas - identity, intimacy, inheritance, and destiny - in your
    life.

Part Two

INTIMACY

Where Am I?

When you have deep intimacy—and you can have it because you already know your true identity—you will experience the Father's presence; and when you experience His presence, you will also abide in His pleasure.

It is important to know God intimately, to have a relationship where you can have face-to-face encounters with Him, hear His voice, see His face, feel His love, experience His presence, and live in His pleasure. If you don't have this kind of relationship, you may find yourself in the Father's house, but you will never feel as if it is your home. You may be in the Father's family, but you will live like an orphan, always trying to earn your place in the family or fill yourself up with things that have already been freely given. You will look for love and significance in all the wrong places. When you have deep intimacy with the Father, you don't hope you've been good enough; you are good enough. The orphan spirit is rooted in fear and scarcity and always has to look out for itself. The son or daughter is safe and secure in an intimate family, and abundance is never in question. The relationship with the Father is based on covenant, and He is a covenant-keeping God. There is no lack in His covenant family. His goodness is a life of intimate fellowship with Him.

CHAPTER FOUR

Papa's Living Room

I spend a lot of time traveling. I love the opportunities God has given me to reach people. I've had the privilege of carrying light into some of the darkest places of the world, and I get to see the faces of people first waking up to the Father's love and learning who they were created to be. As much as I love being on the road, there's something I love even more: coming home. There's nothing like being in that home environment.

I've repeated the homecoming scene many times over the years. I walk into my house with anticipation. There's no fear of being rejected or ignored; I know I'm loved in this place. I'm interested in what's going on in my wife's life, and she's interested in what's going on in mine. We embrace. I hug my children and hang out with the family in the living room. The air is filled with warmth and laughter and affection—all the things that are supposed to be in a family environment. Even the dog is happy. There is no other place on the planet where I feel more accepted.

The home environment isn't always perfect, of course—no one's is. Family members can be a little disconnected at times. Sometimes we experience some friction, and other times we're just doing our own thing. There are times though, like at a homecoming or a holiday meal, when the atmosphere is just right and love flows freely. When that happens, it feels like a little taste of heaven on earth.

Do you know why this environment feels like heaven on earth? Because in a very real sense, it is. It's a reflection of heaven's family atmosphere where love flows freely between the Father, the Son, and the Spirit. We can hardly even begin to understand the kind of acceptance and unity that characterizes heaven, but we were designed to experience it. The Father, Son, and Spirit share their love not only with each other, but also with us. We are meant to live in that atmosphere *all the time*. It's what your heart—and every heart in the world—has always been looking for.

PART OF THE FAMILY

Imagine being invited into God's living room—not for a formal gathering, but just to be with Him, as if you were finally coming home from a long journey. You walk down the hallway with anticipation. You step through the doorway to find welcoming smiles and outstretched arms reaching to embrace you. You have God's full attention as He smiles at you, laughs at your jokes, listens with compassion to your stories, and shows His pleasure in you. You don't even have to ask

Him if He loves you; it's obvious that He does. He never hides His affection. This is the safest place in the universe.

At some point in this wonderful experience, you would find out you aren't just there for a visit. You've been invited to stay permanently. "Make yourself at home," He says. You have the freedom to live in the mansion, get comfortable on the couch, raid the refrigerator, and relax. There is no pressure there; only the Father's pleasure. At first, you wonder if this is real, and a nagging voice in the back of your mind tries to tell you it won't last. But it does. You are part of the family and you begin to feel like it. You can be yourself. You can share your true feelings. You experience so much of your Father's love that you can't help but love Him back. You even start to see yourself the same way He sees you.

You notice that there are other members of the family—your new brothers and sisters—who are always out working. You aren't sure why; your Father isn't the demanding type, and He has servants who do any work He needs. Even when He has tasks for His children, it's so He can work together with them, not so they can work for Him. Yet some toil away on their own. You've also heard of brothers and sisters who left the mansion to find their fortune, but you can't imagine any fortune being greater than your Father's. *Why would anyone leave this place?* you wonder. You decide you're here to stay. It's the most comfortable, reassuring, pleasant place you've ever experienced.

What makes it so wonderful? The Father's love does, for one thing. It's not only His love though that makes it wonderful. It's also because your brothers and sisters fill the living room with love, and honor each other. You've never been in such an uplifting culture, and you don't ever want to leave it. The family gatherings are festive. There are always more gifts than you can count under the Christmas tree—more than anyone would ever need. They are freely distributed, not only at Christmas, but all year long. Eventually you realize how useful these gifts are for the things you want to do. You've seen others take them and develop them into something more. You want to invest in the Father's business too. You love what He does and want to be a part of it.

Sometimes one of the wayward brothers or sisters comes back home, but you never hear a harsh rebuke. They are always welcomed. No one asks questions; they just embrace them and bring them back into the family. They get immediate access to the gifts and take up the family business too. They are home again. So are you. To stay.

That's a picture of our relationship with our Father. Jesus pointed toward it when He told His disciples about the many rooms in the Father's house (John 14:2). He said He was leaving to prepare a place for them in His Father's mansion, but in a sense this is a present reality. We are already seated with Jesus in heavenly places (Ephesians 6:2). We can live in a place of intimate fellowship with the Father, Son, and Spirit *right now*. God's living room is available to everyone. So why are so few people experiencing it? Many people don't know it's possible. Even those who are aware of it may not know how to enter in. They are unsure of their status with the Father. They may know at an intellectual level that they are sons or daughters of the King, but they still aren't certain how enthusiastically they will be welcomed.

Deep down, in the depths of their heart, they don't quite know who they are. They live as spiritual orphans.

WHAT'S MISSING?

A spiritual orphan's heart is always looking for security, affirmation, love, acceptance, value, purpose, and significance because it has never experienced those things from the Father.

Orphans are always trying to figure out what's going on and make sense of it. They are striving to become something because they don't really know who they are. In an orphan world, everybody is looking after themselves because they can never be sure anyone else will look after them. Orphans are always restless and striving.

You can see the orphan spirit in today's headlines and read it in people's eyes. The world is shaking, and people are responding in restlessness. Many are even beginning to trust in fear and believe in it. It doesn't matter to them if 95 percent of their fears never manifest; the "what ifs" are big enough to keep them captive and unsettled. Things have always been shaken, to a degree; the world and its systems have always been restless. But this shaking and restlessness seem to be intensifying. I asked an audience recently how many of them sensed the shaking or were in the middle of a transition. I expected a majority to raise their hands, but the response was actually 100 percent. Practically everyone is experiencing an earthquake. We are living in a very interesting time.

In the midst of their confusion, many people have given up on the idea of hearing the Father's voice—if they ever believed He speaks (or exists) to begin with. Billions are walking around disconnected from the God who made them, unaware of who they were created to be and whom they were created to know and love. Many who do know Him—or at least know of Him— are asking questions. How can we find peace and rest in the midst of the shaking and restlessness? How can we find security, value, and purpose? Who is going to take care of the future? How can we experience a real connection with God? How can we cut through all the noise and hear His voice? In other words, how do we experience the *shalom* we were created for?

YOU WERE MADE FOR REST

We were created to find rest in Papa God. The world, including most of the church, is working hard in order to have a few moments of rest. That is why we see a constant cycle of restlessness around us. We were designed to work *from* a place of rest, knowing our identity as children of God. Our identity does not come from what we do but from who we are. We are sons and daughters of a loving Papa, but many of us live life with an orphan mentality. We may know in our minds that we have a Father, but we are not truly living as His children. *Sons and daughters of God produce sons and daughters of God, while orphans produce orphans.* In the world today, we see hundreds of thousands of orphanages we call churches, and they are producing orphan children. Believers are called to reveal the true nature of God, but we cannot do that with an orphan mindset. We can only do it with a family mindset, with all the love, honor, and unity God designed His family to experience. *Families see promises, not problems.* When sons and daughters arise in the church, the world will begin to see the true nature of God and His family.

Our Resting Place

There is a resting place—the Father's living room, where His family members experience complete acceptance and extravagant love— and I want to help people find it. *People are looking for it on the outside, and they need to discover it on the inside.* The resting place is there, available from God anywhere, anytime. As we will see, you were created and designed to live in it, not once in a while but always. It's where we thrive, receive the promises of the Father, and reign with the Son. It is God's desire for you.

Receiving and Reigning from a Place of Rest

There's another side to the resting place that I want to help people discover too. If you have rest in your life, you can become a resting place for God—a place of habitation for Him. This is actually the key to stepping into your inheritance and your destiny of reigning with Him, and many people aren't even aware of it. Far too many Christians have experienced a visitation from God but have not become His habitation. They are looking to *have* a resting place but not to *be* one. This book is about both—experiencing everything God wants for us by finding a resting place for ourselves and becoming a resting place for Him. When this happens, we receive and reign from that place of rest. This is an invitation into fullness and abundance—and into a Kingdom Family Movement that is now spreading around the world. It is about an entirely different way to see and live.

When we are able to live from that resting place, it doesn't matter how much shaking is going on. Like Jesus, who slept in the back of a boat while a storm was raging, we can find rest in the midst of anything because our eyes are on our Father, who is not nervous about anything. I can know that the One who rules and reigns over the universe is for me, not against me. That doesn't mean I won't experience difficulties—I have gone through many because the enemy is always trying to steal, kill, and destroy—but I know my Father promised abundant life. Anything that comes against me is actually an invitation to get an upgrade into a new level of wisdom, power, and love. I never need to be restless. I can have *shalom* anywhere, in any season because I know who I am and who God is.

WORKING FROM REST

Toward the end of 2015, as I was approaching my 50th birthday, the Holy Spirit spoke to me clearly and said, "Leif, I want you to give me the first six weeks of your year. I want you to start from a place of rest in 2016 so that you can burn brightly without burning out." Despite the challenges in clearing my busy and committed schedule, I wanted to commit to this; it reflects the biblical principle of working *from* rest rather than *toward* rest. As soon as I cleared my schedule and began to prepare for a season of rest, the attack on *shalom* began. Invitations started flowing in and pressures began to mount. My "rest on all sides" became a target for the enemy.

About that time, I had a vision of standing and looking at a huge forest of very big trees in front of me. In the vision, I turned to look behind me and saw many trees that had already been chopped down. I knew this was connected to a shift in seasons: many past accomplishments, but also many things left to be done. As I faced forward again, all I saw were endless challenges, and I felt overwhelmed.

"Do you see this tree?" the Holy Spirit asked, pointing me to one of the large trees nearby. "How long would it take you to chop it down?"

It was huge. "About 10 hours," I thought.

"If you took two hours to sharpen your ax, how long do you think it would take?"

"With a really sharp ax?" I thought. "Maybe about two hours."

Then the Spirit said, "You would accomplish the same, but you would have six hours left over."

Ecclesiastes 10:10 immediately came to mind: "If the ax is dull, and one does not sharpen the edge, then he must use more strength; but wisdom brings success." *I realized it would be much more productive to live wisely from a place of rest than just reacting from a place of busyness.* I began to experience rest as a weapon of warfare—that from a position of rest, we are able to wear the enemy out and reign in areas that once ruled over us. My six weeks of rest that began somewhat restlessly introduced me to a new operating system.

God wants all His sons and daughters at rest in His house. That's one reason this three-chair illustration is so appropriate; you don't work to sit in a chair. You just rest in it. Many believers look for the Father's house as a place of visitation, but God wants us to know it as a place of habitation. The orphan spirit cannot experience that; only those who are sons and daughters can. God sent His Son to become an orphan on our behalf so that we could become sons and daughters. He exchanged places with us on the cross, crying out, "Why have you forsaken me?" to the Father who had always been one with Him. His open invitation is for both individuals and the church to come and abide in His presence. *I believe God is teaching this generation a lifestyle of habitation through family.*

Revivals throughout church history have been Chair 1 experiences—people within the church discovering the identity and intimacy with the Lord. But none of these revivals have been sustained indefinitely because most individuals have experienced visitation rather than habitation. Those who have experienced the resting place as a habitation have not been able to leave that legacy to the next generation.

Our resting and reigning are connected to Jesus. He is in the resting place and is the resting place itself, and we are in Him. He has restored us to what we were given at the beginning of creation. We have to understand what Jesus came to restore—our original purpose in Eden, face-to-face with God and at rest with Him—if we want to experience it. When we are at rest in God, He is at rest in us. When He rests in us, we are complete in Him. We can only receive from Him when He is at rest in us; this union transforms everything. We no longer rest from work, as people in Chairs 2 and 3 do; we work from a place of rest. *The resting place is a lifestyle, and in that lifestyle we begin to reign with Him.* It is the starting point for knowing our Father, receiving our inheritance, and fulfilling our destiny.

> *Whatever we receive in the resting place, we can become.*
> *Whatever we become, we can release.*

THE PATTERN FOR HUMANITY

The fact that Adam and Eve began life in rest tells us that this is our starting point. Their first day was God's day of rest, establishing the pattern for humanity. This theme returns at times throughout Scripture. Noah sent out a dove that kept returning to the ark until it found a place to rest (Genesis 8:9). God established a cycle of rest so we could devote ourselves to sitting in His presence, hearing His voice, seeing His face, and experiencing Him. The Holy Spirit came as a dove to rest on Jesus at His baptism, and Jesus remained at rest in the Father even while He worked. He was able to sleep in the midst of storms because He lived in the resting place. The storms outside of Him had to bow to the peace inside of Him. The night before His crucifixion, He imparted His peace—His *shalom*—to His disciples. It is their right as sons and daughters. Scripture ends with God's people back in His presence, fully experiencing Him face-to-face. This is what we were made for.

THE SEASONS OF REST

There are so many questions when it comes to the topic of resting, and equally as many theories on what resting truly means for each unique individual. In my opinion rest is seen and experienced in two specific ways. The first is having rest or peace of mind; the ability to carry rest with you into any situation or circumstance that might try to overwhelm or distract you. You may be extremely busy physically but in your soul and spirit there is total peace. The other way that rest is experienced is to physically rest—to literally take a pause or a break from all of the noise and chaos going on in your life and to spend a period of time relaxing and refueling. So then that raises the question, what does rest look like for you? Do you need the first type of rest or the second? What if you need both? Where do you even start?

I'm going to ask you to take a moment and use your imagination through this next illustration. Imagine that a large dinner plate is set in front of you. The plate represents your assignment. Then picture this plate as it begins to fill with all kinds of food. The food represents all of the different things that you have to do, need to do, and want to do. Your plate is completely full to the brim so you immediately start devouring this plate. Day after day it seems like the plate is getting fuller each time you begin to eat and after a few weeks at this pace you notice you are starting to carry around a lot of extra weight. The little weight turns into a lot of weight and now even the most minor daily activities or responsibilities that used to come so easily to you are actually becoming extremely challenging for you to complete. You eventually get so exhausted, burdened and overwhelmed that you cry out to God to help you manage this plate. It's too much for you and instead of conquering your assignment, you seem to be further away than you were when you started. The Lord responds to your cries for help and decides that it is best to take some things off of your plate. He shows you how some of the things were never meant to be there in the first place, and how others are just out of season and not satisfying to you anymore. Sure enough, this weight starts to lift right off of you. The Lord puts you through His form of physical therapy and you're able to start not only walking again, but you're even able to run again! You're able to accomplish every single thing that remains on your plate and you couldn't feel any better.

Then one day you sit down and prepare to feast on another perfectly manageable meal, and the plate is full again. After what happened last time you know to invite the Lord in so you cry out again, "Lord, please take these things off of my plate again!" The Lord responds and says, "Oh wait, I forgot something; here, you need this one there too." You are totally confused considering the last time that your plate was this full you got fat and immobile and burned out. You cry out, "Lord, why won't you remove these things?" He responds, "Last time I took all of those things off your plate because you were in a season where you needed to take a pause; you needed to heal and to have time to recover and regain your strength. This time I not only allowed your plate to be full, I loaded it even more because in this next season you're going to need as much nutrition as you can so that you can accomplish your assignment. This time you won't grow fat because I've taught you how to manage your plate; I've taught you how to run and to use all of these things to fuel you toward your goals."

There are seasons where pressing pause is necessary, where cutting back in the areas that God highlights is the only option we have if we want to get back to being healthy. Then there are seasons where the Lord allows our plates to overflow because He is trying to increase our capacity so that we can grow and accomplish more with Him.

WHEN RESTING BECOMES RESTLESS

Years ago I had surgery on my lower back. I had bone fragments that had broken off and were damaging my sciatic nerve. My family has a history of back issues, but to be honest I know a lot of the pain I live with today comes from lack of pausing to rest. My back pain had been severe for a long time but I thought I couldn't take anything else off of my plate. I had too many responsibilities to God, myself, my family, my office, my ministry, and even the world. If I took a break it looked like things around me would start falling apart and I couldn't afford to lose any of the ground in any of those areas that I had gained. I had so much on my assignment plate and I knew I couldn't keep going the way that I was, but I couldn't decide what could come off the plate.

I had the surgery, and for the next four weeks I was required to stay home and rest. You would think that I'd be relieved because obviously rest was what I really needed. At first it was nice to be at home and to relax. Life forced me to remove things from my plate. I was happy to sleep in for the first time in years, to have days that weren't filled with meetings and conference calls, and to not have to hop on a plane. It was wonderful for a time but it didn't take long for my rest to start turning into restlessness.

I was so used to taking care of people, spending my days jumping from important things to even more important things. Sitting at home and watching seasons of my kids' favorite shows while lying in bed didn't feel like I was accomplishing any important life-changing moments. I started to realize that I was so used to having my plate full that anything close to a normal portion felt like I was on the strictest diet! I thought this experience was just trying to teach me to rest physically, but it started to reveal how much more I needed to learn to rest in my soul and spirit.

Those next few weeks were filled with times of going to the root of each area of my life. I began to shake off the old feelings of shame, performance, and needing to measure up. I started to give back to the Lord the responsibility I had taken on to take care of my family and the families of the world. I found peace again. I was able to just spend time in His presence, learning again about my identity and who He is in my life. I was able to be still and know that He is God, to wake up and pause instead of rushing to get out of the door, to literally stop and smell the roses in my wife's beautiful garden.

This season taught me how to prioritize my plate, how to increase my capacity without decreasing my peace. This is where rest and identity come hand-in-hand. Without rest you miss opportunities to go deep and to take care of yourself. Without identity you don't see the value in investing into rest and your well-being. This is why the journey into living from a place of rest is one that can only be taken with the Holy Spirit. Only He knows what you can handle and what may need to be removed from your plate.

God wants you to come into a place of rest and discover on the inside what you are looking for on the outside. Papa is inviting you into His living room, His resting place, where you, a family member, can experience complete acceptance and extravagant love so that you have more than enough to give away.

CHAPTER FOUR DEVOTIONAL
Papa's Living Room

In Scripture Jesus tells us that there are many rooms in the Father's house and that He has a place for each of us in this house. With this teaching, the matchless Son of God is giving us a metaphorical picture of our inheritance as children of God. God has positions of authority for each of us designed to enable us to reign with Him in this life and the next. When we think in terms of intimacy with God taking place in His "house" – in His "living room," it is easier to imagine we are part of the Kingdom family. God desires that we feel comfortable and at rest and peace in His presence. His "house" is another word for His presence. When we find our home in the heart of God, we are no longer orphans. We no longer have to live on the "street," outside the presence of God. We are welcomed into His living room to enjoy all that is to be found with Him.

FOCUS AREAS

» You were made for rest – when there is habitation versus visitation, restlessness gives way to the *shalom* of God.

» When resting becomes restless – root issues that need healing make us restless.

» Working from a place of rest – learning to live from rest rather than from striving.

REFLECTION QUESTIONS

1. Did you grow up with a home life that was basically warm and welcoming or in a "cold" house that didn't provide the security we all need? How does your answer impact the way in which you relate to God?

2. Do you feel like an orphan on the street or a child in Papa's living room? Why?

3. Invite the Holy Spirit to help you identify any root issues in your life that need the healing touch of your heavenly Father in order for you to receive all that He has for you. If you need assistance beyond what is encompassed in this book, consider engaging with a personal local ministry.

REFLECTION

Spend time reflecting on God's *shalom* – His peace that passes all understanding (Philippians 4:7). Are there habits and thought patterns in your life that tend to take you away from the peace of God? If so, are you ready to surrender them to God so that He can replace them with the mind of Christ?

CHAPTER FIVE
Immersed, Rooted & Grounded in Love

God's deepest desire for us is that we would be rooted and ground in love, that we would know the height and depth and width and breadth of the love of Christ, which surpasses understanding (Ephesians 3:17-19). The Bible says that God is love (1 John 4:16), so we can never be comfortable with God if we don't also get comfortable with love. If we are rooted and grounded in love and experience every dimension of God's love, then we are filled with God's fullness. That's where our intimacy with Him thrives.

In Paul's love chapters in Ephesians, we again see the same order of identity, then intimacy, then inheritance. The next thing Paul writes after this promise of being rooted and grounded in love and filled with the fullness of God is that God is able to do exceedingly abundantly beyond all we can ask or think. In other words, from the place of intimacy, we can ask. From relationship we can move into more than we ever thought was possible, where God's fullness starts to flow out of us. *When you're living from fullness, you're no longer living from measure*. Your supply is beyond sufficient; it's abundant. What was in heaven now flows into earth. All of that comes from having an intimate relationship and being one with Him—seeing what He sees, thinking the way He thinks, feeling the way He feels, and loving as He loves.

EXPRESSING AND EXPERIENCING GOD'S FULLNESS

Once, as I was walking through the Oslo airport, a verse came to mind in the form of a rap. I normally don't think that way, but in Norwegian this verse about being rooted and ground in love (Ephesians 3:17) just came in perfect rhythm. (In English it would have been something like, "Rooted and grounded in love, hey! Rooted and grounded in love, hey! How high, how deep, how long, how wide . . ." and so on like that.) As I was singing this to myself, I started to feel waves of being rooted and grounded in love. When I arrived in the city where I was speaking, I discovered that this was the verse my host was reading for the event. Later, I met different people who expressed this same verse—an Egyptian mother, then back in Oslo a former Muslim from Afghanistan who used to abuse his wife. Each one explained that waves of love had been touching them, and I could see the transformation in their faces. They had glowing expressions. All the time, I was hearing this rhythmic "rooted and grounded in love" in my mind and seeing people experiencing the height, width, depth, and breadth of the Father's love. The fullness was being expressed and experienced.

Love is the center of life that holds all things together. While everyone in Chairs 2 and 3 live in fear and restlessness, we know that "For God did not give us a spirit of fear, but of power and love and of a sound mind." (2 Timothy 1:7 NHEG). As this verse makes clear, when we have the Father's love, we also have His power and wisdom. Life in Chair 1 is lived in the center of love, with power and wisdom extending like wings to each side. Many believers are running after power and wisdom, not realizing the reason that they are not experiencing either one. Love must be in the center. Everything flows from the love that is in the center, our resting place. *We can't have God's power and wisdom without first having His love.*

BECOMING WHAT WE BEHOLD

It is important for us to know when to be love, when to be power, and when to be wisdom. The temptation is to pursue the Father's love in order to get an experience of power or wisdom. As we have seen again and again, intimacy is about loving Him for who He is. That's the invitation of Chair 1. By just being with Him, we learn how to see His face and hear His voice. *We become what we behold,* just as in the garden Adam and Eve saw, heard, felt, experienced, and encountered the Father as those made in His image. They gazed at Him and were like Him. They were one with Him in intimacy. *Our perspective determines our experience.*

What we see shapes who we are. In Chair 1, the Father invites us: "Come be with Me and learn to see what I see. Look in the mirror and see how I see you. Look at the world through My eyes." When you start to capture the thoughts of God, things change. You get a renewed mind. You realize how much He delights in you. It finally sinks in that His plans for you are good, and He wants to prosper you. Faith grows; it comes by hearing, not by having heard. In His presence, it's present and alive. This change can begin to take place in you even in the darkest moments. He replaces the old patterns of your mind with thoughts that are full of love, joy, peace, and more.

You also begin to feel the feelings of God. That may sound strange; many people don't believe God has emotions. Jesus certainly had emotions, including joy, anger, sorrow, delight, and many more. We can ask Him to share His feelings with us. We become internally aligned with Him.

In Chair 1, where you align with God, your spirit is positioned to lead your mind, will, and emotions. In Chair 2, your soul takes the lead over your spirit. Your alignment is critical for your assignment, but if your heart is not fully connected to His, you will begin to perform in order to connect with Him rather than live from the connection you already have. Your oneness with the Father is meant to be much more than a theological position. It's an actual merging of hearts under the control of the Spirit.

LIVING IN ALIGNMENT

Many believers have trouble hearing the Father's voice because they are sitting in the wrong chair. They are out of alignment, living from Chair 2 when they need to be in Chair 1.

Chair 1 represents the kingdom of God with the Holy Spirit resting on sons and daughters who see the face and hear the voice of their Father. When the spirit, soul, and body are in alignment in Chair 1, we can hear, see, and feel the Father. This is why Jesus said His sheep hear His voice (John 10:4, 16). In alignment, we are tuned to hear Him. *Open heavens are often between the ears.*

Chair 2 is the kingdom of self, controlled by what we feel and think. In Chair 2, with the soul as the dominating force, His voice is filtered through our mind, will, and emotions before getting into the spirit. God still speaks, but His voice is mixed in with every other thought and feeling we have. We wonder, *"Is this God, me, or the devil?"* That's always a good question to ask, but it's very difficult to answer from Chair 2. Those three options are so intermingled, and it's hard to tell the difference. Deception is subtle. No one wakes up and says, "I'm going to be deceived today." We aren't aware of it. We don't know that we've moved into the wrong chair. Fear comes in, pushes our buttons, and moves us from our resting place. Discernment is very difficult when every voice seems to be coming from the same place and through the same filters

When we listen for God's voice in Chair 2—even though we aren't sure whether it's His or not, because our soul is constantly questioning and doubting—we hear condemnation rather than conviction. We get vague sensations rather than specific direction, think in terms of punishment rather than discipline, and are unsettled rather than at peace. God's voice is convicting, specific, corrective, and full of life and *shalom*. If we sense condemnation, uncertainty, punishment, and restlessness, our filters are letting other voices speak to our spirit. If peace is not evident within us, we can be sure we are not resting in Chair 1.

Fear and guilt will often turn people away from God's voice. When they believe they did something wrong or fear that they are out of sorts with Him, they think He has turned away from them. They may not even expect Him to speak, and all they hear is silence. If they do decide to listen for Him, their fears will often distort what He says and it comes out as negative. Some people even prophesy from this place. Human instincts tell us we need to do something to get right with God again, and they step up their performance so they can feel better about themselves and get God to turn back to them. That is a self-absorbed, Chair 2 way of life.

How do you get out of that Chair 2 way of life? If you realize you are not hearing Him, know that He is still there and that He has not turned away from you. You have turned away from Him. The problem is in your perceptions. Repent! Change the way you see and think. Insist on what you know: that He is a good Father. Go back to your identity. Know who you are and whose you are. Are you seeing His face? If not, then go back to when you did and start from there. Are you hearing His voice? If not, retrace your steps to find out when you moved away. Anytime you notice symptoms of missing something—feeling His love, experiencing His presence, living in His pleasure—don't try to compensate with Chair 2 tactics. Get back to the place of His love, presence, and pleasure. Align yourself with Him and the atmosphere of heaven. This may be a process, and sometimes it may seem like there's a little bit of hide-and-seek going on between you and God. Keep in mind that a mindset rarely changes completely overnight.

RECEIVING A LIFESTYLE

Sometimes people will tell me they are struggling with sadness (for one example), but if I pray for them to have an encounter with God's joy, they only get an encounter. However, if I can plant in them a seed of joy—or love, or peace, or any other fruit of the Spirit—a process begins of understanding God's provision. I take them on a journey to look in the face of the Father of joy. "Ask, 'Papa, what do You see when You see me? What do You feel when You feel me? What do You think about when You think of me? What do You have to say to me?' Then start speaking out loud what Papa God has to say—'The joy of the Lord is your strength,' or, 'Rejoice in the Lord always.'" *When we enter into a process with what God speaks over us scripturally and prophetically, we get more than an encounter. We get a lifestyle.*

In the wilderness, God's people asked for manna, but the next day they wanted fresh bread again. They lived in day-by-day dependency because that was how they received in that season. When they moved into the Promised Land, they planted. They created gardens. They were still dependent, but they received as a lifestyle. We have to see how the sower and the soil work together—to sow the right seed into the right soil, the right environment, the right heart. Then instead of a one-time encounter with joy, peace, or love, they get access to fruitful trees of joy, peace, and love. They don't need to come back the next day asking for the same thing because they can eat of the fruit anytime.

People often tell me they are waiting for a baptism of love, hoping for it as a single encounter. I would rather give them a process for full-time access. If they can stick with the process for 30 days, they get an upgrade. We have heard amazing stories from people who follow the process for a month.

HOW TO RECEIVE A BAPTISM OF LOVE

» Think what God thinks

» Feel what God feels

» Hear what God says

» And then . . .

» Say what He thinks, feels, and says . . . even when it is very often the opposite of your own thoughts, feelings, and words.

The seeds that God plants in your heart during this time will grow up into beautiful trees that bear fruit. If our relationship with the Lord is moving from one encounter to the next, we will find ourselves looking for something new every couple of weeks to keep us going. But God wants to plant in you a seed of love that can grow deep roots into the soil of love, so you can have a tree of love that feeds you continually. Don't live just for key moments and experiences. Start seeing yourself the way He sees you. Let your roots grow deeper in love so you can receive more love, and your spirit will tune in to His voice. *Rest, receive,* and *be.* Power and wisdom will begin to flow.

OPENING OUR HEARTS TO HIS COMPASSION

When we are in alignment, our mind, will, and emotions are nothing to be afraid of because our spirits are taking the lead. I often ask God to share His emotions with me because I know He is an emotional God, full of compassion, delight, joy, and many other feelings. I did this in a service recently, where I had some Chair 2 perceptions of the people who were experiencing oppression and darkness. When I asked the Father to let me feel the way He felt toward them, I moved into a Chair 1 encounter with Him and the Spirit came upon me and broke my heart for them. I could see the oppression and persecution they had been experiencing, how they had been abused and enslaved by the culture. A strong sense of compassion rose up in me for my brothers and sisters. I sensed a holy anger for how the enemy had been messing with my family in this oppressive country. Then something began to break. The atmosphere changed, and many people who had been feeling the weight of oppression a few moments earlier began to sense something new. They got a taste of the Promised Land. More than 80 percent of the people we prayed for in that meeting got healed, and most of the hundreds who were there had needed healing. Miracles began to flow easily. It started with me capturing the sensitivity of the Holy Spirit, sensing Jesus' fellowship with those who were suffering, and opening my heart to His compassion.

Why did things suddenly begin to flow? Because as sons and daughters who have an intimate relationship with the Father, we learn to do what He is doing and say what He is saying. Our hearts become tuned with His. We realize we are seated with Christ in heavenly places. It's a very intimate place to be. *When you are in the Spirit, the things of the kingdom—righteousness, peace, and joy in the Spirit—begin to flow through your life.* This is how we reign as transformers of society and culture.

One of the most significant miracles I have experienced is one I didn't actually get to see. I was in a meeting when the presence of God began moving and people started pushing toward the stage. The night before, two quadriplegic boys were healed and began to walk, so a Muslim father had brought his son to the meeting. He kept holding up the wheelchair and then setting it down, then he would hold up the boy and set him down. This continued for some time; he was desperate for a touch but could not get up to the stage with all the people pushing their way forward. Security would not let us go down to him. Finally guards came to take us out because we might have been crushed by crowds if we continued. I saw the father from a distance alternately holding up the boy and then the wheelchair, and I tried to point in his direction. My heart was broken for him. I knew they were thinking if they could get prayer, the boy would get well. That was their hope.

When we finally left the area and got to a safe place, I just sat there very overwhelmed and emotionally drained—first by the goodness and kindness of God in all the things we got to see, but also by what we were not able to see. Later, the coordinator of the event got a call from a person at the meeting who told the story of this father and son, the Muslim man who had brought his 12-year-old son to the meeting in hopes that someone would come and pray for him. When they left, he was very depressed. He had hope, but nothing happened. Throughout the night, the presence of Jesus continued to linger over the boy, and he started to feel tingling in his body. Waves of God's presence touched him, and by morning he was feeling everything. He walked into the kitchen and hugged his father. When I heard this story, I realized that even when it seems like nothing is happening, Jesus can heal people. His presence lingers and continues to heal. We had felt God's emotions for this father and son, and He encouraged us with the hope of what He does when we are not able to see.

ENCOUNTER BRINGS ALIGNMENT

I have had a lot of back and neck injuries and surgeries. Once, when I got a herniated disk, I received several prophetic words about healing. "Wow," I kept telling myself, "God is going to heal this. I'm going to feel better!" I was really excited. I continued traveling during the next season as I always have—a healing school with Randy Clark in England and other conferences all over the world. I had to get an injection in a hospital in Thailand because I could no longer walk with the pain. That helped, but the pain was still excruciating, and I didn't want to go back on opiates again. Somehow the grace to keep going was there day by day, so I stood on my promise of healing and kept going. Right before a big Planetshakers event, I collapsed. Doctors looked at the MRI and told me I would be paralyzed if I didn't have surgery. They showed me the picture. I was so disappointed, but what could I do? I couldn't walk. I couldn't really do anything. I have a high pain tolerance, but the pain felt like a knife was sticking in me constantly. Because I had believed in my healing, I had gone too long without help. I still have nerve damage in my leg because I kept walking on it so long. So I cancelled upcoming events and had surgery.

Six days after the surgery, I was lying in bed and feeling a little disappointed with God. I didn't question whether He was good, but I did wonder how He has so many friends if this was how He treats them. I was disappointed I had to cancel events on short notice, disappointed in how that affected my ministry, disappointed that I was still in so much pain as I recovered. While I was lying there, I heard God confirm my thoughts. "You seem a little disappointed with Me," He said.

"Yeah," I thought.

"You thought you were going to get healed."

"Exactly."

"Because you had all these words that you were going to get healed."

"Yeah, I did."

"I don't do second-class healings. Who said you are not going to get healed?"

I immediately thought back to a specific word of knowledge that I was going to be healed. Someone had come up to me and said, "Your lower back. L4, L5." It was very clear.

"If you had been healed, you would be happy," God said.

"Yes, I would."

"So many people prayed for you."

"Yes, many people. I would be very happy if You had answered their prayers."

"I don't do second-class healings," He said again. "Son, you know Me well enough to know I took you aside right now and you entered the hard work of rest. I chose to use a surgeon with the skill set to bring healing, just like bringing you someone with a word of knowledge."

I repented. "I'm so sorry, Lord. I don't see the way You see, think the way You think, or feel the way You feel. There are things I just don't understand."

After that moment of repentance, I had an encounter. It's hard to explain, but I felt like I was being taken up, and then suddenly I could look down at the world. This lasted more than two hours. I was lying in bed, but I was traveling through the universe. I would think of places like Albania or Pakistan, and then I was there. I knew I was thinking the way He was thinking. I saw things from His perspective. I began to feel His heart. I still feel the impact today from this one encounter in His glory and presence, face to face. It brought an enormous shift in how I saw myself and how I saw the world. Where I once saw problems, I now saw promises. I recognized an invitation to partner with Him in the promises. If I had not had that encounter, I would not have been able to see, think, and feel like He does, and I would not be able to do what I am doing. It established an understanding and a pattern for aligning with His thoughts, feelings, and perspectives.

"In the next season, you're going to love you the way I love you," He said. "You're going to burn brightly without burning out." Many of the things I am walking in today came because of this season of healing. It changed things. I learned how to position myself regarding victory. *We live from victory, not toward victory.*

The essential keys in Chair 1 are resting and receiving. Intimacy cannot come any other way. In that place of intimacy, what you behold, you become. What you become, you release. *You receive love, become love, and then release love.* This was the plan from the beginning. It is what Jesus restored for us.

Because we are one with Jesus—He is in us, and we are in Him—we are seated with Him in heavenly places (Ephesians 2:6). That's where Chair 1 really is. This is the Spirit-filled life Jesus demonstrated on earth. From that position in heavenly places, we can bring heaven to earth as He did. We are free of fear and able to love with power and wisdom. We walk with divine purpose and a supernatural lifestyle. When intimacy with God is our highest priority, we become trustworthy to walk these things out. Just as He encountered me in my hospital bed—a place of rest—and spoke so clearly, He comes to each of us to give us His eyes and make our hearts beat with His. In that unity, in that resting place of union with Him, we are ready to receive an inheritance.

CHAPTER FIVE DEVOTIONAL

Immersed, Rooted & Grounded in Love

The apostle Paul wrote a beautiful prayer for the believers in the church in Ephesus that sprang from his awareness of God's marvelous provision for us (Ephesians 3:14-20). Verse 17 is an expression of the Father's deepest heart desire for us - that we would be rooted and grounded in love, and that we would know the height and depth and width and breadth of the love of Christ, which surpasses understanding. As we experience the fullness of God's love we become rooted and grounded in this love to such an extent that we begin to live from a place of love instead of measure. Love becomes a lifestyle that opens our heart to His compassion so that we can live from victory in Christ instead of toward victory.

FOCUS AREAS

» Learning to love God for who He is – instead of what He gives.

» Living in alignment – the kingdom of self versus the Kingdom of God.

» Receiving – a lifestyle and a baptism of love.

» Opening our hearts to His compassion – led by the Spirit, not our emotions.

REFLECTION QUESTIONS

1. Where are you when it comes to loving God for who He is versus what He gives?

2. If self is on the throne in your life, how can you go about dethroning yourself and allowing God to take His place of authority over your life?

3. What are the five ways to receive a baptism of love?

REFLECTION

Scripture tells us that Jesus healed from a heart of compassion, and that Jesus is an exact representation of the Father. Therefore, God has a heart of compassion. In light of these truths, find some of the scriptures where Jesus is healing out of compassion and then reflect on why it is so important to open your heart to God's compassion.

CHAPTER SIX
Power, Love & Wisdom

I was given a beautiful watch on one of my visits to Pakistan. One afternoon when a jewelry store was about to close for prayer, I went in to have a couple of links taken off because the watchband was too big for me. I saw two young, radical-looking Muslim men when I walked in. It was not a very welcoming atmosphere. My past tendency would have been to slip into a Chair 2 attitude and operate out of fear. However, I had just talked about the sensitivity of the Holy Spirit and had to remind myself that the Spirit is not just in me but upon me. If He is always with me in the here and now, the atmosphere does not have to change me. He can change the atmosphere. That is the power of our connection with Him.

Both of those boys were pretty rude to me, and my instinct was to get out of there. It was very uncomfortable. They stared at me with their dark eyes and spoke to each other in Urdu through their long beards. I left my watch to be repaired and planned to come back some time much later after the afternoon prayers. When I returned, one of the guys said, "Excuse me, but the manager wants to see you." Then a nice gentleman came out and was a bit more friendly. He introduced himself and told me the owner wanted to see me. *Am I in trouble?* I wondered. The watch had been a gift, and I assumed there was no problem with it. I couldn't imagine why he wanted to see me.

When I got to the back room, I saw a picture of the president of the nation. This owner was a general in the army, but he owned several stores. "Could you sit down for a moment?" he asked. "Who are you and where did you come from?"

I introduced myself but didn't know what else to say.

"Earlier today when you were in the store, I don't know what happened, but something came in and filled my office here. I went out and asked the people in front if they had felt it. I asked them who was in here. They told me it was just a blond-headed, blue-eyed infidel. I told them that when you came back in, I wanted to meet you. So what is this?"

I knew very clearly what he had experienced: the Prince of Peace. And blessed are the peacemakers, for they are the sons and daughters of God (Matthew 5:9). This is one of the byproducts of intimacy with the Holy Spirit. Out of your life will flow love, joy, and peace, and sometimes those things will be tangible to people who are unfamiliar with them. The Spirit also fills us with His wisdom and knowledge, and I got a word of knowledge for this man. I listened to what the Holy Spirit had to say about what was going on in his life and was able to minister to him and pray with him. He gave me a business card and a beautiful pen that I carry with me as a remembrance that when we walk in intimacy with sensitivity to the Spirit, He flows from us to bring the environment of heaven into earth.

THE OVERFLOW OF INTIMACY

Clearly, intimacy is not confined to our relationship with God. He has invited us into a covenant relationship to become one with Him, but we have to take that same culture that exists among the Father, Son, and Spirit and apply it to our human relationships—to become one with our spouse, to have intimacy in our families, to be humble and vulnerable in our friendships. This is why John wrote that it's impossible to love God and not also love others (1 John 2:9-11; 3:10-15). *If we are saturated in the environment of heaven in our relationship with the Father, Son, and Spirit, we will also live out the environment of heaven in our relationships with other people.* Intimacy is meant to spill over into other areas of life.

In John 15, Jesus connects pruning with intimacy. He makes it clear that He wants to abide in us and for us to abide in Him. "I am the vine, you are the branches," He told His disciples (John 15:5). But a good gardener goes into the garden to prune branches for maximum growth. Jesus says the Father does that with us (John 15:2). Why? So we will carry more fruit. A friend once told me that it's beautiful when he sees a tree that is full of fruit, but he also knows that it has been stripped naked and made vulnerable through pruning. When he sees the nakedness of a tree, he sees as much beauty there as he does with a tree full of fruit. In both cases, the love of the Father is made manifest. Remember that when you feel barren and naked. *In humility and vulnerability, authority begins to flow.* You are being pruned in order to carry more fruit, more authority. He will take you deeper in order to take you wider and higher so you can be entrusted with more. As you become a resting place through intimacy, you bear the fruit of your Father, and it's beautiful to see.

ABIDING IN THE FULLNESS OF INTIMACY

The ultimate purpose of our intimacy is union—oneness with the Father, Son, and Spirit.

My spiritual son, Paul Yadao, and I had just arrived to speak in a city in southern Asia that had made headlines from some recent attacks. These were stormy times, and tensions were running high. After going to our hotel room, Paul and I realized we had some storms and tension within us too. We knew there was nothing we could do out in the city until God had done something inside of us, so we put on some soaking music in the room and spent some time enjoying the presence of Jesus. We marinated in His presence, welcoming Him in with His love. Soon we felt a blanket of peace come down from the top of the room and cover us, and we could hardly move. It was that kind of peace that passes understanding, guarding our hearts, minds, and bodies. We felt not only that we were at peace but that we had *become* peace—almost like we were a blanket of *shalom*. There were no more storms. Nothing had changed outside that room, but everything had changed inside us. We left and were taken by security guards to the cricket stadium where we were speaking, and thousands upon thousands of people were there. We could sense the fear and tension they were feeling, but when we walked up to the stage and looked over the multitudes, we sensed the peace in us beginning to leak out into the stadium. It was a phenomenal sight; the same blanket of peace that came over us in the hotel room came over the crowds. From that moment on, there was a supernatural grace to speak, testify, and release signs and wonders. God began healing bodies in that environment of peace. What happened inside of us affected what happened outside of us. The One we had been with was the One who was being released. The One we beheld was the One we became. The One we had become was the One we were now able to reign with.

LEARNING HOW TO RECEIVE

Soaking has become a popular practice in Christian culture over the last few years. Some people entering into soaking for the first time ask, "What do I need to do?"

"Nothing," I tell them.

"How do you do that?"

"You don't," I say. They struggle with that idea because we are in the habit of doing something in order to get something. But in God's kingdom, receiving is the only way to get something.

Sometimes we soak for two or three hours with no agenda other than just experiencing Him. Often, heaven is so attracted to the Christ in us in those times that we enter into an experience of oneness that is hard to describe. We become a resting place for the Dove. We know that from that place we can start our assignment because there has first been proper alignment. Many people try to go straight to the assignment, and they don't have the anointing of the Dove for it yet. But when you have that, you are like Jesus coming out of the wilderness with a message: "The Spirit of the Lord is upon Me because He has anointed Me" (Luke 4:18). You have good news in the middle of bad news, light in the middle of darkness, healing in the midst of sickness and disease, joy in the middle of sadness, dancing in the place of mourning, and beauty in the place of ashes. Whatever the issue is, you have something to offer from heaven. You represent a good, good Father in a world that needs Him. That's what the gospel is all about. Jesus actually prayed this for all His followers in John 17:

> ". . . *that they may be one*, even as we are one; I in them, and
> you in me, *that they may be perfected into one*; that the world
> may know that you sent me, and loved them, even as you
> loved me." (John 17:21-23 WEB, *italics added*).

Jesus is praying that His disciples would be one with each other, and also that they would be one with Him—in the same way that the Father, Son, and Spirit are one. There is no closer unity than that. We are in Him, and He is in us—a relationship that Paul emphasizes again and again in his letters. The picture and phrases of "in Christ" and "Christ in us" throughout the New Testament tell us that we are called to something even more than a face-to-face relationship. It's oneness. We aren't just sitting across the table from God, or even in His lap. We have been united with Him. True rest in the kingdom is an overflow of this union of our spirits with God's Spirit. It's a covenant of love that forever binds us with Him.

RESTING, RECEIVING, REIGNING

In order to be about the Father's business, you must be rooted and grounded in love, knowing who you are and whose you are.

Chair 1 is a place of identity, and it is also a place of intimacy—or "into-me-see," where you open yourself up to be seen. From that covenant of oneness, there's responsibility, and we will see how an inheritance is available for us and a destiny awaits us. However, we could not jump to those things without first doing the hard work of rest and entering into a place of knowing our identity and cultivating our intimacy. This is where we rest and receive so we can then reign with Him.

Chair 1 is a lifestyle of humility because it involves realizing that without Him, I can do nothing (John 15:5). What I do comes from my unity with Him. This isn't a false humility, because I also acknowledge that in Him, I can do all things (Philippians 4:13). That's where we get our confidence and courage. He gives grace to the humble, so in humility I can always find grace to do all things. In

Chair 2, self and pride are in the center. It's all up to me and what I can do. There's no grace available in that situation, so I have to strive and struggle and sweat. In Chair 1, I come in and recognize I'm one with Him. Jesus could do nothing without the Holy Spirit, and He could only do what He saw the Father doing. He lived from a place of intimacy; that's where His power flowed from. Every member of the Trinity was fully aware of what the others were doing. We have an invitation to experience the same.

Never mix up the order of resting, receiving, and reigning. If you live from Chair 1, you will see the culture changed because the culture of heaven will manifest through you and anyone else who has learned to abide in unity with Him. People who have journeyed into intimacy with the Father, Son, and Spirit have learned to live life like they have a home. They have recognized the invitation of the Father and have a place in His living room. When you get comfortable in that space, knowing that He adores you and delights in you, you can just enjoy being with Him, knowing you're doing exactly what you were created for. Love flows from people who have learned to be intimate with their lover. *Instead of looking only for the presence of His promises, you begin to look for the promise of His presence.* That's where the kingdom flourishes in your life. What begins in rest leads to reigning with Him.

"God had a dream and He wrapped your body around it."
Bill Johnson

My wife and I have four children, who, as you know, all come from acts of intimacy. In order to have that kind of intimacy, you also have to have nakedness . . . and vulnerability . . . and humility. But when you become united with the one you love, there's a seed, an impartation, and life forms. You go through the process of carrying the life He has placed within you. With our Lover, that can be a dream that He shares with you, a secret of His heart, a revelation of His personality or His purposes, or anything else He is willing to implant in His beloved ones. And He shares them in the secret places of intimacy. Ephesians 1:4 says God chose us before the foundation of the world, which means He knew us before the foundation of the world. All things that exist are designed to be God-centered; they are from Him, through Him, and to Him (Romans 11:36)—including you. When 50 million sperm cells were on a race toward an egg cell, He knew you would win the race. You were in His mind. So who were you before the foundation of the world? What is it about you that made you significant to Him? What is unique about the ways you can know Him and appreciate Him? There is no one in the universe who will see Him and worship Him exactly as you do. You were brought into this relationship not only in love but also in the Beloved (Ephesians 1:4, 6). You are the Father's dream. Amazing things happen in your life when you realize that the best thing about God is God Himself—enjoying who He is and just being in His presence as a fulfillment of His dream.

TRUE INTIMACY – FACE TO FACE WITH GOD

I began traveling around the world when my children were very young. It was an exciting time as I had launched my ministry and started to experience open doors and favor in my life, and yet it was also the most challenging time for me and my family. Being away so often was very painful for us. While I was experiencing incredible things around the world the most incredible things in my world were back home.

Since being away from my family was such a challenge I decided that the time I did get to spend with my wife and my children should be memorable. For anyone who knows me knows that my number one love language is giving gifts, so I began a tradition called daddy dates. When I was home, each of my children would get to pick their favorite places to go, their favorite places to eat, and get to shop for their favorite things as if it was the biggest birthday of their lives. One memory that stands was our visits to an arcade that all of the kids loved. It had everything you could imagine - a carousel, swings, arcade games, dancing games, and more. Since all of the kids loved the place, we would sometimes do joint daddy dates there. I would buy them all of the coins that they could ever want and they'd split up and find their favorite games and I'd take turns watching each one do their favorite activity. After hours of play we'd head downstairs to the cafe where a friend of mine was the owner and he'd let the kids pick any of their favorite sodas and treats. In that season orange soda was always the popular choice and they were so excited to get to have as many re-fills as their little stomachs could handle. When we were done there we would usually visit the local mall and shop, or step next door and go to the movies. It would be a day full of celebration, playing, some arguing, bonding, and we would all leave with unforgettable memories.

These dates happened often, nearly every time I was home. No matter how many dates, my kids never grew tired of the fun places we would go and the new things we would try, and to this day, the daddy dates are still incorporated in our time together. I'll be honest, there were times I'd wonder to myself, *Would they still want to spend time with me if I weren't able to give them these fun things?* I just wanted to know that their love and affection toward me wasn't orange soda induced. I noticed a tendency with my children for shopping to take the center place in our relationship. As soon as I would get home, they would greet me and say they loved me. Then soon afterward, they would ask when we were going to go shopping—almost as if they were saying, "I love you, Daddy, but here's what I want you to do for me." They wouldn't have used those exact words, of course, and I know they really do love me, but children are quick to notice what they can get out of a relationship.

I remember very clearly one time when one of my daughters came to me and said, "Dad, I love you." I was touched, of course, but I kept waiting for a request. I wondered what she wanted. It turns out that she didn't want anything. She just wanted to be with me and love on me. I even asked her, "Do you need something?"

"No, Dad, I just want to be with you."

Do you know what that does to a father's heart? It moved me and made me feel a deep connection with her. It made me want to know her heart even more. We spent some time together, and before long I found myself asking if she wanted to go shopping! I made the offer; she didn't even have to ask me. I wanted to get her whatever she wanted.

I think that's exactly what God has in mind when Psalm 37:4 says to delight ourselves in Him, and He will give us the desires of our hearts. Instead of focusing on His gifts, we realize that the best thing about God is God, and the best thing about Jesus is Jesus. When we come to Him with nothing but requests, He is gracious and often answers us, but that ends up being the extent of the relationship. When we come to Him just to be with Him, however, His heart bonds with our heart, our desires blend with His, and He enjoys satisfying our desires, sometimes without our even asking. That's what happens in intimate relationships. Connected hearts seek to meet the needs and desires of the other.

The beautiful truth about my relationship with my children is that they love me, not what I give them. If anyone in the world at that time would've asked my children (and many did), "If you could have anything in the world what would it be?" they always responded "Just to have our daddy home." They would share how their fondest moments were waking up to me sitting at the breakfast table and going to sleep at night knowing that I was in the house just a few feet away, in the room with their mother. That beautiful truth has resonated in me since those early beginnings. It taught me a lesson about identity teaching us what true intimacy is.

My prayer for you while you are reading these pages is that you continue to go after the supernatural things, that you continue to attend the conferences, revival meets, and healing services, that you always hunger to experience His goodness and celebrate the things He's done in the land of the living. When the celebrations are over and you are driving home or thinking of what is next, my prayer is that when Father God asks you if you could have anything, your answer would always remain, "I just what to know that You are home with me"—to know that He is at the breakfast table when you wake up in the morning, to know that He is in the house when you go to sleep at night, that you will forever be grateful for the daddy dates that He loves to take you on knowing that nothing compares to just being with Him. When your heart's desire is always to have Him close, you know that you've crossed over into intimacy territory.

CHAPTER SIX DEVOTIONAL
Power, Love & Wisdom

At the start of this chapter I shared the story of how, when God's presence was released into a hostile environment, it ushered in Jesus – the Prince of Peace. This is an illustration of the power, love and wisdom of God in operation. I was able to carry a strong presence of God with me because I had learned how to live in the overflow of intimacy that comes from relationship. I was able to experience God's peace in the middle of a storm because I invested time beforehand in the place of resting and receiving. Developing this kind of a lifestyle is not easy but it can be done. Your investment of time with God will yield immeasurable Kingdom benefits.

FOCUS AREAS

» The overflow of intimacy – the intimacy you experience with God will flow from you to others.

» Abiding in the fullness of intimacy – go deep with God.

» Resting, receiving and reigning – the fruits of going deep with God.

» Opening our hearts to His compassion – led by the Spirit, not our emotions.

REFLECTION QUESTIONS

1. How much time do you invest in a lifestyle of intimacy with God?

2. We all find it difficult to devote extended time to soaking in God's presence in the midst of our daily lives. What are some of the roadblocks in your life to soaking with God?

3. Cultivating intimacy from a place of vulnerability and humility can be scary but necessary. Why is this?

CHAPTER SEVEN
Home Again

Between Eden and Jesus, not many people got to experience the Father's living room. Some, like prophets, priests, and others who were sensitive to His Spirit, got an occasional glimpse. Many heard about what it must be like to experience that wonderful place. There were revelations; God was making Himself known. But entering in? Centuries went by when people longed for His presence and only got an occasional taste. Only a few ever experienced an open heaven. For most, the environment of Eden was faint hope. Yet God had already put a plan in place before the foundation of the world. He was on a mission to restore His family.

THE RESTORATION

*Jesus represented the first time since Eden that a human being was
totally one with the Father in a covenant of love.*

God became flesh and dwelt among us (John 1:14). Jesus was 100
percent God and also 100 percent man. His identity was as a natural
son of Joseph and Mary and as the Son of God. When He was 12,
His parents took Him to the temple in Jerusalem to celebrate Passover.
Joseph and Mary left town assuming He was in the traveling party,
but they realized along the way that He was missing. They had left the
anointing—the meaning of "Christ" is "anointed one"—behind in
Jerusalem. When they returned to the city, they eventually found Him
in the temple, astounding the teachers with His wisdom. He could
have started His ministry right there and then, but it wasn't time. Yet
He was already in His Father's house taking care of family business.
He knew who He was.

For the next 18 years, Jesus continued to place Himself under
the authority of His human parents, becoming a carpenter. The
language suggests He was learning to be a master craftsman. He
learned His father's skill, honored and loved His parents, became one
with their vision in covenant with them. By the time He was about 30,
everyone knew this son of Mary and Joseph was a master craftsman,
ready to take on the family business.

But the heavenly Father intervened. Jesus went to be baptized
by John the Baptist, not because He needed the baptism of repentance

but because He came as a man for us to follow and enter into His footsteps. As He came out of the water, the dove came down as a picture of the baptism of the Spirit. The Father spoke from heaven, "You are My beloved Son; in You I am well pleased" (Luke 3:22). There were three baptisms going on that day:

A Baptism of Water

A Baptism of the Spirit

A Baptism of Love

The Father spoke words of affirmation and delight over His Son, flooding and saturating Jesus in His pleasure and promise. Jesus had been faithful in the natural; He was about to enter a ministry marked by the supernatural. He would change the world from the place of rest in His identity and intimacy with the Father.

As we've seen and will explore in more detail later, His sonship was tested. After His baptism, Jesus was immediately led by the Spirit into the wilderness where the enemy who twisted Adam and Eve's identity in the garden now tried to twist Jesus' identity too. "If you are God's Son . . . ," he said, and then tested Him in three areas each of us will be tested in too. If you pass the test of identity as Jesus did, you will come out of the wilderness as He did—able to say, "The Spirit of the Lord is upon Me, because He has anointed Me" (Luke 4:18). That's a Chair 1 statement, the starting point for everything we do.

Jesus might as well have said, "This is who I am, devil, and there's nothing you can do about it." He had the Father's blessing, and He knew it.

Everybody was in awe of Jesus' teaching because they were witnessing the Word in the flesh. They could experience heaven coming to earth. They were so familiar with Jesus as the natural son of Joseph and Mary—that's how they knew Him—that they did not know how to honor His anointing or His identity as the Son of God. They missed the revival God would have given to Nazareth right then and there. He had to go to other towns where He would be recognized as a prophet and eventually as the Messiah.

Jesus came in with the value system of heaven. He did only what He saw the Father doing and said only what He heard the Father saying. He lived the part of a beloved Son in whom Papa God delighted. He showed the world what God looks like and how God loves. Sinners were very attracted to Him. The ones who struggled the most with Jesus were the religious and political leaders of the day. He chose 12 disciples to enter into a covenant relationship with, and then three within those 12 for a particularly close relationship, and then one among them who was the closest. He created a family and raised up the spirit of sonship over them so a generation of blessing could begin to flow.

IDENTITY

When we begin to recognize who Jesus is, we begin to recognize who we are.

Again and again in the gospels, we see Jesus' identity being discovered by His followers and questioned by His critics. It's the central question of His ministry. One of the central stories that demonstrates this theme is in Matthew 16:13-20, when Jesus asked His disciples, "Who do people say the Son of Man is?" (NIV). That is a big question even today among the Chair 3 world—Muslims, Hindus, Buddhists, atheists, agnostics, everyone. You'll hear many different answers to that question: a good guy, a good teacher, a prophet, a martyr, and more. Then Jesus asked His disciples, "But who do *you* say that I am?" Simon got a revelation from heaven and went from a Chair 2 perspective to a Chair 1 perspective. "You are the Christ, the Son of the living God"—the anointed one and the Father's Son. When Simon said that, he became a rock. He saw Jesus' true identity and stepped into his own. He became unshakeable. Jesus said He would build His church on that unshakeable foundation, on the revelation of His identity, and the gates of hell would not prevail against it. Not only that, Jesus said He would give His followers the keys of the kingdom so they could loose and bind according to heaven's reality. He gave them authority.

Do you see the progression? Simon Peter proclaimed Jesus' identity and began to see his own identity as Jesus declared it to him. Then he and the other disciples received an inheritance of authority so they could bring heaven to earth. Jesus said He would build His church on this revelation—His identity as the anointed Son and the identity of other anointed sons and daughters of God. When we know Papa loves us and that His Spirit rests upon us, and we are able to rest in that identity and fellowship, we become unshakeable. Jesus builds His church and gives the keys of the kingdom to those who know who they are.

THE JOURNEY HOME

God's Spirit is going after His children to bring us into the intimacy
He desires for us.

If Jesus was who He said He was—the beloved Son of God, the anointed one—why were sinners and tax collectors, some of the most unpopular people in the world, attracted to Him? That question was one of the biggest stumbling blocks in the minds of the religious and political people of His day. They challenged Him on this point on many occasions, and on one of those occasions, Jesus told three stories that demonstrate a Chair 1 perspective.

The first story, found in Luke 15, is about a shepherd who leaves 99 safe sheep to go after one lost one. From a Chair 2 point of view, that doesn't make much sense. It isn't good economics to go to so much trouble for a 1 percent loss. But from a relational, covenantal, family perspective, it was the only option. For all of us who have been lost sheep, aren't we grateful that God is like this shepherd? Our stock goes up immediately when God places that kind of value on us. We are not a commodity; we are sons and daughters, precious members of the family, beloved by a God who delights in us. The judgmental religious people understood that this was a story about Jesus Himself. He is calling Himself the great shepherd and connecting Himself to the God of Psalm 23. God goes after those who need to be rescued. This is how He thinks.

The second story, found in Luke 15, is about a woman who had 10 coins and lost one. Jesus has just compared God to a shepherd, and now He compares Him to a woman. Many people see feminine characteristics in the Holy Spirit, which should not be much of a stretch for us when we consider that both male and female were created in God's image (Genesis 1:27). He is a nourisher, a caretaker with a sensitive, loving heart. The parable about a woman who lost a coin sheds a different light on who God is and what this heavenly family of the Trinity is like. Again, there is great value placed on the thing that was lost, which reflects God's attitude toward the sinners and tax collectors who were drawn to Jesus.

From what we know of church history, I believe these parables are connected to three reformations: the doctrinal reformation of the 1500s, the Holy Spirit reformation that began in the early 1900s, and a reformation of love that is unfolding right now and giving birth to the Kingdom Family Movement that we are experiencing. In this case, the woman, who can be seen to represent the Holy Spirit, reflects the outpouring of the Spirit in the second reformation that began over a hundred years ago, as God's Spirit pursues His children.

THE PRODIGAL SON FROM CHAIR 1

The highlight of Luke 15 is the third parable, one of Jesus' best-known illustrations of the Father's heart. A Chair 2 perspective calls it the parable of the Prodigal Son and focuses on the failure of man rather than on the faithfulness of a loving father. Sometimes when I teach this parable, I describe it as a story about a father with three sons, and everyone in the audience looks at me as though I'm crazy. But it really is. One of the sons was rebellious, one was religious, and the other was telling the story about His two brothers and His Father. All were in the family—they are called sons, not sinners—but the first two had a Chair 2 worldview.

The rebellious son had an orphan heart focused on looking out for himself: "Give me, give me, give me." He didn't understand his identity and didn't have an intimate relationship with his father, but he insisted on receiving his share of the family wealth and ran away with it. Asking for an inheritance before the father's death would be offensive in any society, but especially so in a Middle Eastern culture. He wanted his share. Sons and daughters had been killed for much more minor offenses than this. It was extremely dishonorable. But the father honored his request and gave each of the sons their share of the estate, even though inheritance is meant for mature children. The rebellious son was not mature at all, and he took his inheritance and wasted it.

Those of us who do not come from a Jewish background may not grasp the disgrace of this story, but this son ended up tending pigs—an unclean animal that Jews are forbidden to eat and that the religious leaders listening to Jesus' story would not even go near. The rebellious son ran out of money, all his friends left him, and he was destitute. In our day, it would be like the son of a wealthy family ending up as a homeless heroin addict desperately searching for his next fix in alleys and slums. This son is as far from the father as a son can get. The religious leaders would be so outraged at this character that they would stone him if he were there.

At the end of his rope, the boy comes to his senses and decides it would be better to be a servant in his father's house than a son in a distant pigpen. He doesn't really repent—we see regret but no sorrow for how he broke his father's heart. He expresses no remorse about how he violated the covenant of love, rebelled against his father, and dishonored the community. He is still thinking about himself and what course of action would be in his best interests. As he is heading home and rehearsing the lines he is going to repeat to his father, Jesus says the father saw him from a long way off. I imagine the father was looking every day, hoping his son would return. When he saw him, he did the unthinkable for a man of his stature in that culture. He ran. That means he lifted up his robes and showed his legs—an extreme show of indignity. He got dirt and mud on his feet—a dishonor normally reserved for servants and slaves. Why did this father run? Not only was he eager to see his son; he may have also wanted to prevent an honor killing. Such a son would have been an offense to the entire community. The father didn't want the villagers to stone him. He had to reach him first.

The father didn't run away from his son's sin; he ran toward it.

When the father got to his son, he did not rebuke him, strike him, insist that he be cleaned up from his contact with pigs before touching him, grudgingly accept him back under certain conditions, or anything else Jesus' listeners might have expected. He embraced him and kissed him—just as if he had never done anything wrong. A Chair 1 perspective knows that you overcome evil with good and that it's the kindness of God that leads to repentance. He embraced the mess and the smell of pigs. He even put the family robe on this filthy young man. He offered a robe of righteousness and relationship to cover the rags of unrighteousness and offense.

Jesus doesn't say so, but this might have been when the son began to break down. Repentance—*metanoia* in Greek—is a shift in the way you think and then, as a result, in the way you live. When you see this kind of unconditional love and acceptance, you begin to think about yourself the way God thinks about you. You start to love the way He loves. His love does something to you. You don't want to go back to the pigpen again. You want to stay in the resting place, in the Father's living room, where you have everything you need. This is about much more than dealing with sin and rebellion; it's about undoing the root of the orphan heart. That's what God's love goes after. Again, the Father wants His family back.

THE RESTORATION OF CHAIR 1

I believe we can see the three reformations and the restoration of a Chair 1 worldview in this parable. The robe is a picture of justification by faith—the first reformation. After the father puts the family robe on his son, he gives him the family ring, a symbol of identity, intimacy, and authority. Then he puts sandals on his feet so he can walk as a family member in the shoes of peace. He even throws a party for him and kills the fatted calf—a symbol of covenant. Immediately upon his return, the son has already been justified and given everything he needs to represent the father's house. He has the robe of righteousness, the ring of identity and authority, the sandals of peace, and a celebration of the relationship. He has found rest—a restored identity, intimacy, inheritance, and destiny—and has become a resting place for the Dove.

The story isn't over though. The older brother was out in the field when his younger brother returned. He was not in a resting place; he was busy working for the father. He was *doing* so he could *have* so he could *become*. He didn't even want to be in a family relationship with his brother; he calls him "this son of yours" rather than "my brother." He can hardly believe that his brother has squandered his inheritance and yet his father still says, "All that I have is yours." He does not have the same rebellious spirit the younger son has. Instead, he has a religious spirit. That spirit gets offended when people come in off the street and immediately receive the Father's favor. He is like Christians who say, "I have been in church all of these years, I've been faithful and filled with the Spirit; I've been serving You; Lord. Why are You doing good things for these people and not me?" Even though this is a different spirit from the rebellious spirit, it still comes from an orphan heart. It was there in the beginning—the "knowledge of good" in the tree of the knowledge of good and evil. The younger son went after the "evil" branch of the tree, while the older son went after the "good" one. Yet it was still the same tree. This brother was doing all the right things for God, but he did not know how to work from God. He was in a restless place because he did not know how to be a son in the father's living room.

God is not after servants – He desires relationship. He wants a living room full of sons and daughters who know how to simply be in His presence.

God already has multitudes of angels who can serve Him 24 hours a day; He doesn't need or want servants. He wants relationship—sons and daughters to fill His home. The father in Jesus' parable pleads with his older son to come back in the house where there is fullness and joy in the father's presence. The refrigerator is full. The living room is a place of delight. He doesn't have to work to be a son there; he can just be one because that's already who he is.

This is what the biblical story is all about, from Genesis to Revelation. God wants His children—both the rebellious and religious ones—to come home and enjoy His fellowship. Yes, there are things to do and responsibilities to fulfill, but this relationship begins first and foremost with identity.

Who are you? I hope the first answer that comes to mind is a son or daughter of God. Not a servant, a minister, an employee, a student, a spouse, or anything else that makes you feel like you are performing a role. Millions of people are out there doing the work of the kingdom in order to prove to themselves and others that they are important in the kingdom. All of them were already important on day one. You were made in the likeness of God. You became a son or daughter when you believed. Your identity was already fully established. You will never be satisfied chasing after identity in what you do and what you have. You can only do and have from the identity you already have—if you know who you really are as an anointed son or daughter of a good, good Father. *You can only experience the kingdom from a place of rest.*

CHAPTER SEVEN DEVOTIONAL
Home Again

Jesus represents the first time since Eden that a human being was totally one with the Father in a covenant of love. In Jesus, God literally became flesh and dwelt among us (John 1:14). He still dwells among us in the power of His Spirit as Christ in us, the hope of glory (Colossians 1:27). Jesus' baptism in the river Jordan was the moment in which His identity was revealed. Notice that as soon as His identity was established, Satan came and tried to destroy that identity. This is a picture of what happens to each one of us – Satan wants to destroy our God-given identity so that we cannot fulfill our Kingdom destiny. If we can recognize who Jesus is and understand His identity, we begin to recognize who we are. Once we understand who we are, we can begin the journey home to the heart of the Father. Kingdom living begins with identity.

FOCUS AREAS

»   The baptism of Jesus – water, Spirit, love.

»   Prodigal sons and daughters – moving from chair 2 to chair 1.

»   Three reformations – the robe, the ring, the sandals = covenant restored.

»   Opening our hearts to His compassion – led by the Spirit, not our emotions.

REFLECTIONS

Spend time reflecting on the three baptisms that took place when Jesus was baptized – the baptism of water, the baptism of the Spirit, and the baptism of love.

Examine the three reformations highlighted in the story of the prodigal son: the robe, which represents justification by faith, the family ring, which is a symbol of identity, intimacy and authority, and the sandals that allow the wayward son to walk as a family member in the shoes of peace. Reflect on these three reformations as they apply to your own life. Write down what you hear God saying to you during this reflection time.

Two parables from the book of Luke, chapter 15, are used to teach on three reformations: the doctrinal reformation of the

1500s, the Holy Spirit reformation beginning in the early 1900s, and the reformation of love that is currently unfolding. Reflect on the impact of the first two reformations – access to the Word of God, and encountering the Holy Spirit – upon your life thus far. How could a new reformation that releases the love of the Father influence the world through your life?

PART TWO SUMMARY REFLECTION:

INTIMACY

Where Am I?

In chapter 4 we examined the concept of living as beloved sons and daughters of God who are always welcome in the Father's living room. This "room" is a place of rest close to the heart of God where our restlessness gives way to God's rest. When we work from this place of rest, striving gives way to receiving. Chapter 5 speaks of God's deepest heart desire for us – to be rooted and grounded in His love so that we can receive all that He has for us. Rooted in Him, we are in alignment, with hearts open to His compassion. Chapter 6 talks about intimacy, the fruits of intimacy, and the importance of vulnerability and humility in the life of believers. Chapter 7 begins with Jesus as our restoration, bringing us back into a covenant of love with the

Father. Using examples from Scripture, we learn about identity, and relationship.

ACTIVATION

» Identify areas of restlessness in your life, and then think about the times when you have been able to come into a place of rest with God. Develop a plan of action for moving from restlessness to rest that you can put into practice in your day-to-day life.

» Make a list the "fruits" that have come from those times when you have been able to come into a place of rest with God. Next, commit to setting aside a time to rest in God's presence daily for one week. At the end of the week, note the fruits of your time with God. It may be helpful to identify those areas of your life where you need to build in healthy margins for rest to include stopping, receiving, recharging, and realigning.

» Prayerfully consider how you might be more vulnerable with God.

PART THREE

INHERITANCE

What Do I Have?

Only those with the right identity as sons and daughters, who are living in intimacy with the Father in His home, can experience the inheritance that is available to them.

I read a story about a man who was a multi-millionaire but spent his life scavenging in the streets because he was constantly afraid he might not have enough. He could have lived a life of abundance, but his fear would not let him. That's how many Christians live. We hope to step into our inheritance without realizing we already have it. We live toward our inheritance rather than living from it. We look forward to the inheritance we will receive in heaven without any awareness of heaven's resources that are available to us now. It really is possible to receive a kingdom inheritance now and draw on the resources of heaven. How? By knowing who we are and whose we are. When we experience the inheritance that is available to us, we become a resting place where heaven is attracted to the Christ that has found a home in us.

Many believers don't know the fullness of their inheritance. God has poured the spirit of sonship into our hearts (Galatians 4:4-6) and, like the father of the prodigal son, assured us that all that He has is ours (Luke 15:31). We are in the family, and therefore we share in the family inheritance. Jesus is the Son who inherits nations (Psalm 2:8) and for whom all things were made (Colossians 1:16). So this is a pretty enormous inheritance—all of heaven and earth; Jesus inherits every bit of it; and we are co-heirs with Jesus (Romans 8:17). God has blessed us with *every* spiritual blessing in heavenly places in Christ (Ephesians 1:3). There is no lack, no shortfall, no limit in these promises. Rooted and grounded in love, we can know the love of Christ and be filled with the fullness of the Father, who can do exceedingly beyond all that we ask or think (Ephesians 3:14-21). He offers us the extravagance of His riches in glory.

This inheritance is already yours, but your access to it comes through intimacy with the Father. Being intimate with Him reveals His heart toward you. You are a family heir. He has given you all good things in your inheritance. You received this not by doing something but simply by being, knowing who you are and who He is. As you learn the family business, the family inheritance is released to you in increasing measure.

CHAPTER EIGHT

Heirs of God

LEARNING TO VALUE OUR INHERITANCE

When we value something in the kingdom of God, we steward it.
When we steward what God has given us, we can multiply it.

A friend of mine is a wealthy businessman who bought his wife an incredibly gorgeous diamond ring. It was huge—it looked like she was wearing a house on her finger. One night they had several guests over to their beautiful home to experience her cooking, which is amazing in itself. They love entertaining, and she makes some really phenomenal meals. As the guests were coming in and enjoying the art collection in their home, she thought about the ring. She had taken it off to prepare the meal but wanted her guests to see this wonderful gift she had been given. She looked for it and couldn't find it. She went through the trash, and it wasn't there. Later, they looked through every trashcan in the house, searched every corner, pulled out drawers, and went to great lengths to find the ring. Finally they found it, but it had taken quite a bit of effort. Why did this search take so much of their focus and energy? Because of the ring's value. They were willing to do anything that was needed to recapture what was valuable to them.

It is vital for us to understand what is available to us. It is worth our focus and energy. God has provided a heaven full of resources that He wants to see His sons and daughters bring to earth. Everything in Papa's house is ours. It's our inheritance. Many people wonder why we see so little of it, but one of the reasons is that we do not know how to value it. If I gave my wife a diamond ring but she thought it was a cubic zirconium, she would probably not take great care of it. It might end up in a pocket or a drawer. However, if she knew the value of it, she would guard it carefully and store it somewhere safe. One of the reasons we write such small checks from our heavenly account is that we don't know the value of what we've been given.

WHAT WE HAVE

Because we know our identity and our intimacy with the Father, we can now talk about inheritance. Many people want to go directly here, and some jump from church to church looking for signs of their inheritance while never finding their identity in the Lord or going deep with Him in intimacy. However, now that we have laid a foundation and put first things first, we can focus on what we have been given. Having looked at who we are and whose we are, we can now look at what we have as heirs of the Father's estate. The economy of God's estate does not look like the world's economy.

The Father's Estate

»   Chair 1 thinks in terms of inheritance.

»   Chair 2 things in terms of profit and loss.

We can recognize in the stories of Luke 15 a strong connection with inheritance. In response to the questions of the religious and judicial leaders about why so many Chair 3 people of the world were drawn to Jesus, He [Jesus] began with a parable of a shepherd who left 99 sheep behind to go searching for a single lost one. A Chair 1 perspective says, "That's good economy; go after the lost one. We're all family, and we can't lose any members." A Chair 2 perspective says, "Why are you leaving us for a stray? It's only one. We need you." One view thinks in terms of inheritance, the other in terms of profit and loss. The second parable of the woman with the lost coin is another example of a stewardship issue. A woman with 10 valuable coins has lost one of them, and she goes to great lengths to find it. Jesus is telling us that this is how God stewards and takes care of things.

In the parable of the prodigal son, both of the sons are focused on themselves and on their share of the estate. You will find this spirit very often connected to inheritance; orphan hearts value God, a spouse, a boss, a friend, or someone else for what that person can give them and how that person can bless them rather than for who that person is. Many churches are filled with a "bless me, give me, fill me" attitude today. It's very important to notice that the father did not give these sons their inheritance. He gave them a share of the estate, a portion of his livelihood (Luke 15:13). On the surface, that might appear to be the same thing, but there's a subtle difference. An inheritance is tied to maturity, so the father didn't give his rebellious son everything. He gave him a portion to steward. The son left the father and lived extravagantly. In today's terms, we would probably say he partied it away. He indulged in an awful, rebellious lifestyle and ran out of money. This Jewish boy wasted everything and ended up in a pigpen. He strayed as far from the father as he could. *An orphan spirit lives toward inheritance; a spirit of adoption lives from inheritance.*

HONOR

As we honor roots, we will be entrusted with fruits.

Something was missing with this boy, and it's also one of the biggest missing pieces with regard to our inheritance today: *maturity.* A Chair 2 perspective keeps us in immaturity, away from our inheritance. It's a spirit of entitlement. You will see it in business, government, and even ministry. "One day I'm going to be the boss." "Someday I'll replace the senior pastor." There needs to be honor. When we value God, we value people. When a father or mother has worked hard for something and made provision, a son or daughter needs to show honor. Honor is what love looks like. That sense of value will result in stewardship, that stewardship will result in multiplication, and that multiplication will result in authority. Many of us today have received gifts and blessings from above. How we deal with them will determine how we will be entrusted with heavenly riches.

I have tried to make honor a part of my journey. I honor my parents; I have honored the schools that I came from—my elementary school teachers, Sunday school teachers, all the people who have had influence in my life. I asked my parents how, out of 34 family members who came to the U.S., 31 of them are confessing, born-again Christians. That is a lot for a national heritage where only 7 percent of the country claims to be born again. I was told I had a great-grandmother who knew how to pray. Generational blessings have flowed from her prayers.

I went back to Norway to honor my roots. I sought out the family of a man who was one of the biggest keys to Norway's freedom, morals, and blessings today. Most people don't know who he is, but the fruits of his life are still evident. His family was a little surprised when I came to them and asked his great-great-grandson to bless me, but I got to experience some of what their great-great-grandfather paid for with his faithfulness. By honoring those who have gone before me and poured into my life, directly or indirectly, I get to stand on their inheritance. It's an overwhelming experience to take responsibility for inheritance; we get to spend what someone else actually paid for. A life of honor extends those blessings and passes them on to the next generation, so that our ceiling becomes the next generation's floor. I have begun to see significant increase in favor in my own life by honoring what others have already invested.

The rebellious son in Luke 15 mishandled his inheritance and dishonored his father. He didn't have a right to take what belonged to his father and waste it. When he got to the end of his supply and found himself eating the pigs' food, he realized how much better it was at his father's house. He was still thinking of himself. Like a heroin addict who has run out of drugs and gone into detox, a basement apartment with a little food and basics starts to look pretty good. He wasn't sorry about wasting everything. He simply felt the consequences of his sin.

Now we get to the inheritance part of the story. You'll recall how the father ran to him and gave him a robe, a ring, and sandals. He had been looking for him every day; that's how he was able to see him while he was a long way off. He loses all sense of dignity and extravagantly shows his joy and affection. His son has been lost and now is found. When the older brother complains, the father replies, "all that I have is yours" (15:31). The inheritance is there. It has been there all along. The father has not been withholding anything. He is simply waiting for his sons to become mature enough to move in their inheritance. *Some people have favor with God but not with men; others have favor with men but not with God. Sons of blessing and inheritance have both, just as Jesus did* (Luke 2:52). Favor flows on both levels for those who are mature enough to receive it and walk in it.

THE RING

You will get to heaven with a robe, but you will not bring heaven to yourself until you've got the ring.

The first half of this book was about *the maturity of knowing our identity and becoming intimate with the Father.* Many who sense that their value system is God-centered—people who are involved in ministry or have done their best to live up to God's standards in marriage, family, and work—may still be focused on self. It's very subtle when we begin valuing God and others for what they do for us rather than who they are. This kind of thinking is rooted in an orphan heart. God wants to deal with your root issues so you can have an encounter with His love, be set free, come into His presence, get your identity back, and enter into intimacy with Him.

That's when the Father puts the family robe and ring on you and says, "Now let's talk about inheritance. I have an estate, and I want you to be part of the estate planning. You can steward what I have and multiply it, and we will fill this earth with My glory so people will know I'm a good Father." He is inviting you into the light business, and your assignment is to invite light into every dark corner of the world. He wants us to do this in partnership with Him, but only from a place of maturity. We have to be trustworthy with our inheritance.

We've seen how the robe represents justification by grace through faith alone. It is a robe of righteousness. That's the invitation for anyone who is struggling with sin issues. All sin takes us away from the Father, but He clothes us in a robe of righteousness so the villagers and even our own hearts will not condemn us. Everything we've been looking for can be found at His home in His presence, a place of security, love, value, purpose, and affirmation that we receive in intimacy with Him.

The second thing the father gives the returning son is the family's signature ring. From this moment on, he moves into a different level of inheritance. Many believers have a robe and can say, "I'm righteous. I'm a son, a daughter, and so I'm a co-heir with Jesus. This is what's true of me!" And it is true, but until you have the ring, you do not have the inheritance. The robe transforms you from a sinner to a saint; the Father sees it and sees righteousness. The signature ring allows you to represent your Father. When you go into the store with that ring, you can sign for anything. It means the Father is responsible to cover your expenses.

A SPIRIT OF ADOPTION

A spirit of adoption lives from inheritance.

Everyone in Chair 1 or 2 has a robe. Only those in Chair 1 know how to use the ring. That's because an orphan spirit is based in fear, but a spirit of adoption is based in faith and rest. Many who have a robe look forward to their inheritance one day in heaven. Some may even keep striving for their inheritance on earth. The good news of the kingdom is that the inheritance has already been provided. We can begin stepping into it now if there is genuine repentance that shifts the way we think, so we see ourselves as the Father sees us and then understand, value, steward, and multiply what we have been given. The Father is a sower who plants a seed in good soil. That soil is a heart, and goes directly to our heart issues. Then we can have the heart of the Father for others, and capture the heart He has toward us. That's the first step in being entrusted with inheritance.

From the moment the Father puts a ring on our finger, we can live from a spirit of adoption. He is saying, "Here is the master key to the safe. I can trust you with it because you have My heart as My son or daughter. The son in Jesus' parable had always been a son, but he was a rebellious son with self at the center of his life. When his father gave him the ring, he had responsibility to steward his father's estate. Based on his regret of his past experience, he would no longer have any desire to squander his father's wealth. He would invest it and represent his father well. *When we get a revelation of who we are and whose we are, we have no desire to return to anything else.* We realize we have a responsibility to represent our Father, to loose and bind things in His kingdom. We wear the ring with understanding.

THE YOKE OF SONSHIP

Wherever we step, we are royal priests who represent the environment of heaven.

After the robe and the ring, the Father puts sandals on us. This is not cheap. The shoes of peace were bought with a price. They are beautiful sandals. People with inheritance walk in the shoes of peace. They are the blessed peacemakers who will be called sons of God (see Matthew 5:9). Isaiah 9:6-7 tells us that the government of the kingdom will be upon the shoulders of the Son, and His government, His peace or *shalom*, will never stop increasing. That's why He invites everyone who is weary and heavy laden to come to Him. His burden is light (see Matthew 11:28-30). This is a yoke of sonship, a royal priesthood in the Father's Kingdom. It's a government in which we find our rhythm with the Son to represent God before the people and represent the people before God.

This is the purpose of inheritance—that the sons and daughters of God who have found rest with Him and are becoming a resting place for Him will walk in *shalom* with Him and rule with Him. In every step we take, we have the opportunity to represent *shalom*. We translate this word as "peace" in English, but it has the sense of much more—of the wholeness, completeness, and fullness of the Kingdom. We are raising up peacemakers in this generation to be ministers of reconciliation and culture changers who know how to walk in the right sandals, who walk not before or after the Father but with Him. By resting in Him, we are seated with Him in heavenly places (see Ephesians 2:6) ruling with Him from the Father's throne. He paid the price; we step into His inheritance as king.

This is how David went from being an anointed shepherd boy to Israel's king, and then passed his reign to his son. He paid an enormous price so his son could rule from a place of *shalom*. Solomon inherited peace because his father was always at war. He was able to build a temple and a palace and to flow in wisdom because of the environment of peace David passed down to him. In 1 Kings 5:4, Solomon remarked that he had peace on every side, and because of that security he was able to build, a city was transformed, and kings and queens came from all around to see and experience the fruits. That is what we want to see in our homes, churches, businesses, cities, and nations. The rest of the world comes to see the *shalom* and the wisdom that flows from it. This is the environment of heaven we are able to represent on earth.

COVENANT NOT CONTRACT

At the end of the story of the prodigal son we find the celebration that the father gives the returning son. It is a covenant meal because *inheritance comes from a covenant*, not a contract. A contract is conditional, based on what each party does. A covenant is based on who we are. It implies an unconditional relationship. We are one with the Father and in covenant with Him, not based on our performance but on our identity. Once we have become one with Him, the invitation is there for us to enter into the party, the covenant, where we live not from measure but from fullness.

The older brothers in our world today still have a core value of doing in order to have and then become. "We are out here working," they say, but they are still missing the point. They are achievers and not receivers. The father says, "Son, all that I have is yours. You could be in My presence in My home every day. The refrigerator is full. I have servants working out in the fields all the time. All I want with you is to come in and be with Me, but your value system has driven you outside. You are not defined by what you do. Why don't you come home? Stop performing. Stop trying to accomplish things for Me. All that I have is yours. I have a heaven full of resources that are available to you. Come spend time with Me, and then when we go into the fields, let's go together."

Older brothers see lack. They see another brother eating more than half the pizza, and they worry about not getting their fair share. They don't realize that the Father owns the bakery. There will always be enough. There is no competition, no unfairness in a home where the Father owns more than enough and shares it freely.

This was a major shift in my own life. I used to live from measure, from limitations rather than abundance, and going to the nations was a problem to be achieved. I know this story so well because it was my own story. I know how it is to be a prodigal son and a prodigal's brother. So many times I wondered, "Why did this person get blessed and not me? Why did that person get healed but I didn't? I've been faithful, I've been studying, I've been praying. I've stood in line all over the world waiting for people to pray for me to have these blessings. I've done all these different things, and here comes this guy off the streets getting all these good gifts—open-heaven experiences, miracles, all the things I've been longing for." My heart and my attitude were focused on me and my lack.

God has prepared a wealth of inheritance for those who love Him. We did nothing to achieve it; we can only receive it. That's the way it always is in the kingdom. Chair 2 people are achievers, so they try to get the inheritance. In Chair 1, the inheritance gets you. It is available without measure for those who will learn how to steward it.

Paul wrote that we have received "not the spirit of the world, but the Spirit who is from God, that we might know the things that have been freely given to us by God" (1 Corinthians 2:12). There are no limits to what we have been freely given: "Eye has not seen, nor ear heard, nor have entered into the heart of man the things which God has prepared for those who love Him" (1 Corinthians 2:9). It really is an amazing promise, but it also leads many believers to wonder why they are not experiencing such extravagance. The reason is that many people do not understand the dynamics of inheritance.

THE NATURE OF INHERITANCE

We have to train our eyes to see our inheritance in terms of destiny.

If I pointed to a patch of soil where seeds had been planted and said, "What do you see?" many people would say, "Nothing." However, if you looked a little closer, you might see a seed. Where some people see a seed, others see a future tree, and others see even beyond that to a forest, or maybe even a paper industry or an orange juice industry. That's because some of us only see what is in front of us, while many others of us recognize and value the potential that is there. We need to understand what is available to the sons and daughters of God from heaven's resources.

Jesus told a very interesting parable in Mark 4:13 and said something unique about it: that if you don't understand this one, you won't be able to understand the others. This parable is a picture of three S's: a sower, his seed, and the soils it falls into. The point of this parable is that the harvest we get depends entirely on the kind of soil the seed is sown into. You can have the best sower in the world and the most powerful seed there is. The potential is there. However, if the seed doesn't fall into the right soil, if it isn't in the right environment, then you aren't going to have fruit. We have to understand the dynamics of inheritance. To put it more positively, if we understand, then value, then steward, and then multiply, we get authority. There's a connection between knowing our inheritance and taking responsibility for it, and it's a very important connection to remember. *What we do not understand, we don't know how to value. What don't value, we will not know how to steward. What we don't steward, we will not be able to multiply, and whatever we don't steward and multiply, we don't have authority over in that area.*

The father in Luke 15 made a very significant statement to his son: "All that I have is yours" (Luke 15:31). That is the Father's gift to us. It's what He has restored. He provided for everything in Jesus' finished work on the cross. What is true of Jesus is now true of us. He inherits all things (Hebrews 1:2), and we are His co-heirs (Romans 8:17). That means we inherit all things with Him.

The first part of Ephesians explains this beautifully. God has blessed us with every spiritual blessing in heavenly places (1:3). He chose each of us long before the world was ever created, and in love,

He calls us holy and blameless (1:4). That is already settled. He adopted us as sons and daughters to be part of His family (1:5) and made us accepted (1:6). He has freed us from sin, not for us to struggle to be barely free, but to be completely and abundantly free in Christ (1:6-10). Then, in unfolding His will for us, He has given us an extravagant inheritance (1:11) and guaranteed it with the Holy Spirit (1:13-14), providing for everything we will ever need and bringing us into His plans. His guarantee means He will finish this work in us.

Paul prays for a spirit of wisdom and revelation so that we know the hope of our calling, the riches of our inheritance, and the greatness of God's power for those who believe (1:15-21). Why? Because inheritance is for the mature. I told my children when they were young that when they were old enough and mature enough to drive, I was going to give them a reliable, high-quality car. I didn't want to worry about them breaking down by the side of the road in the middle of nowhere while I was away speaking in some other country. I wanted to do this for them. I'm a man of my word; when they were old and mature enough, the car was there. It took many years of learning responsibility and understanding the value of a car and how to care for it before the car became theirs.

If you give an inheritance to children who are not yet mature enough for it, it will harm them rather than help them.

Many of us go through the frustration of knowing positionally who we are in Christ and what our inheritance is without fully experiencing it yet, and we wonder what has gone wrong. Nothing is wrong. We are in that period of promise, when we know what we will be given but are growing in maturity to be able to handle the responsibility. If God gave us all of our inheritance up front, we would be like 10-year-olds with car keys. We would not be able to handle the weight of our responsibility.

A 16-year-old named Callie was the youngest person in the United Kingdom ever to win the lottery in 2003, and she lost nearly all of the £1.9 million on plastic surgery, drugs, and parties. She was driven to despair, and at one point she even contemplated suicide. Today she is much happier, studying nursing and living a more normal life.[1] Her story is not unusual; studies estimate that anywhere from 30 to 70 percent of lottery winners declare bankruptcy within a few years.[2] Why? Usually because they begin investing in depreciating assets like cars and trips; they give money away recklessly to family and friends; they fall for high-risk investment schemes that don't work out. The same dynamic applies to people who inherit a lot of money from parents or other wealthy relatives. People who suddenly come into wealth often do not know how to handle it. They either have not been trained or do not have the maturity to steward what they did not work for.

---

1 http://www.therichest.com/rich-list/poorest-list/10-lottery-winners-who-went-broke, accessed April 2, 2017.
2 http://fortune.com/2016/01/15/powerball-lottery-winners/; http://www.cleveland.com/business/index.ssf/2016/01/why_do_70_percent_of_lottery_w.html, accessed April 2, 2017.

INVESTMENT NOT EXPENDITURE

In God's kingdom, He trains us for inheritance and authority. *He is doing something in us so He can get something to us.* He is willing to get as much to you as He can also get through you. He does not want to give us our inheritance as an expenditure. It's an investment. It is building toward something. We are to take our inheritance and bring it to another level.

In Norway, where I am from, many people had nothing during World War II. Businesses and homes were taken away from them while the country was occupied by Germany. In the years after, I saw how my parents worked hard to give me what they never had. We see this again and again where one generation builds a family business and raises up sons and daughters to take it over. If the children understand and value what their father and mother did, they steward the business and multiply it. The ceiling of the parents becomes the floor of the children, and they build on it further. This happens in business, ministry, and many other areas of life. There are pastors and teachers who lay a foundation for their children to build on, and if the children understand and honor what their father has done, they can receive what they have been given but also increase its capacity. It becomes a legacy, not an expenditure. This is how inheritance operates.

There is quite a difference between children of blessing and children of inheritance. People with a Chair 2 worldview are after a blessing. There's nothing wrong with that in itself; we all love being blessed by the Father. Children of blessing will take inheritance and eat up the harvest. They don't understand what Mom and Dad have sacrificed, that others planted and did all the work. They benefit from the harvest without understanding how to increase it. The result is a wasted harvest, sometimes over several generations.

Children of inheritance know how to steward and invest. We are not looking to use up the harvest as an expenditure. We are looking to increase it for our own generation and future ones. We enjoy all the resources from the Father's house, but we understand that there is a purpose behind them. We take responsibility toward fulfilling that purpose. We see the relationship between our inheritance and our destiny—and the destiny of generations to come.

KINGDOM FAMILY MOVEMENT

You cannot go out and get your inheritance; it has to get you.

Much of the church today is pursuing inheritance as something to be achieved rather than received. Though the heart behind this pursuit is often good, there seems to be a lack of understanding. Many believers read promises of inheritance and claim them without realizing the context of identity and intimacy, or the purpose of destiny. They just go straight for the Father's goods.

Everything in the kingdom flows from relationships. It can only be received. You will find that this is true in every area of your life with God. It is not about productivity, service, principles, or anything else that feels impersonal. It is about family love, family relationships, and growing the family business. The kingdom is a family business; orphan hearts cannot receive it and would not know what to do with it.

The only way for inheritance to happen is to find your identity in being a son or daughter of the Father and pursuing intimacy with Him simply because He is. Everything with God is relational. This is why the two key themes for finding rest are "covenant" and "kingdom." One is about the relationship we live from, and the other is about the Father's purposes. Heaven on earth was a family business from the beginning. That's what we saw in Eden until the serpent's orphan spirit infected Adam and Eve's perception of their Father. Now what we see in Chairs 2 and 3 looks very similar: seeking purpose without the relationship, being self-focused rather than God-focused. When we come into Chair 1, our hearts align with the Father's. We become one with Him. We see as He sees, feel as He feels, and think as He thinks. From there, we can know what is available because we will use it as He does. Then we can go and do what we are called to do.

CHAPTER EIGHT DEVOTIONAL
Heirs of God

God desires that we live from inheritance instead of toward it. Through Jesus, He has made heaven's resources available to us now. Yet, so often we don't understand the value of what is available to us because we think in terms of profit and loss rather than inheritance. God is looking for mature sons and daughters whom He can honor. How we deal with the gifts and blessings we receive determines how we'll be entrusted with heavenly riches. There is a connection between knowing your inheritance and taking responsibility for it. We must work our way through the period of promise to the place of the maturity of knowing. God intends for us to live from abundance so that we can freely give what we have freely received.

FOCUS AREAS

»   The Identity Thief – the age-old lie that began in the Garden.

»   The Truth Deficiency – identity confusion violates the Kingdom family culture and leads to an orphan spirit.

»   Recognizing Lucifer's Strategy – to keep us from intimacy with God.

REFLECTION

Regarding the nature of inheritance, 10 scriptures are highlighted that help us to understand the dynamics of inheritance. Spend time reflecting on each of these scriptures, making note of what God is saying to you. Pay attention to how God uses scripture to teach us how to make our way through periods of promise to places of maturity.

Reflect on what the concepts of the Kingdom Family Movement mean in your life and how you can become more a part of this family.

CHAPTER NINE
Children of Inheritance

When Elijah was about to be taken up into heaven, Elisha followed him from city to city and would not leave his side. When the two crossed the Jordan and Elijah was preparing for his dramatic exit from this world, he said to Elisha, "Tell me, what can I do for you before I am taken from you?" (2 Kings 2:9). The only thing Elisha asked for was a double portion of Elijah's spirit. Elijah told him that was a hard thing; the power Elijah walked in had cost him a lot. Nevertheless, the request was granted, and Elisha went on to do twice the recorded miracles that Elijah had done.

Today people ask for a "double portion" pretty casually. I've had people come to me and say they wanted a double portion of the power, wisdom, or love I'm walking in, but they do not understand the relational elements—the identity and intimacy—that I have fought for and learned first. The places Elijah traveled on his last journey had symbolic meaning: Gilgal, where Israel's circumcision took place when they entered the Promised Land; Bethel, where Jacob experienced an open heaven by resting on a rock, even though he did not want to be there; Jericho, where Israel was first tested in battle in the Promised Land and their hearts were tempted. Elijah had been through many tests. Though he had freely received an inheritance, he had paid a price for the maturity required to steward it. Elisha was willing to suffer the cost too. He receive a double portion because he knew what a double portion implied—that he would be honoring and stewarding an inheritance for his generation and the ones to follow.

LEARNING TO VALUE WHAT YOU RECEIVE

The process for my daughter to receive a car from me took time. She was a daughter of blessing, but it took time for her to become a daughter of inheritance. What's the difference? A blessing is something the father has paid for. He feeds his children, buys them what they need, and takes care of everything for them. There's a season for that. As a child matures, the father's gifts become less about blessing and more about the family wealth. Is she mature enough to steward what I have worked for over the years? Does she take responsibility? Will she use what she has been given for a greater purpose—to expand it, multiply it, or invest it—rather than simply spend it? That's how a child becomes a son or daughter of inheritance.

We see this with Jesus and his natural parents. He didn't just learn how to be a carpenter; He became a master craftsman. He mastered His father's skills. His heavenly Father translated that responsibility into a much different and much more significant inheritance than his family was about to give Him, but Jesus had demonstrated in both realms that He could be entrusted. He would be faithful to steward the supernatural and inherit the kingdom.

It is interesting in Luke 15 that the father of the rebellious and religious sons treated them as sons of inheritance before they had shown the necessary maturity. He said, "All that I have is yours," while they were still acting like orphans. It's normal as a child to value a father for what he can do for you, but sons and daughters eventually grow out of that. They realize they are being given access to something someone else paid for, and they learn to honor it and value it. They take what fathers and mothers have worked hard for and then build on it.

We have to go through a process of maturity so that we will handle the inheritance we receive in a way that helps us and does not hurt us. That is why the Father can say, "All that I have is yours," and it still is not in your hands yet. It is yours—to inherit, but perhaps not yet to possess. You must learn to value what you receive so you can steward it well. *Whatever you know how to steward, you know how to multiply. Whatever you multiply, you have authority over.* The parable of the seeds and the soils teaches us to see not just a seed but a 30-fold, 60-fold, or 100-fold harvest. We can't just ask for what someone else has without going through what they have been through. You may be able to access their inheritance, but that only comes as you honor the relational elements they have experienced.

Your Father does not want your blessings to take you away from the One who blesses you.

I've seen many people tap into the inheritance of a spiritual father and move in that power and fruitfulness for a while, then decide that they don't need that mentor or father anymore. They don't realize that one of the reasons they were able to access the blessing was by being under that person. When we know how to honor inheritance and take responsibility for it, we can build off what others have paid a price for. We take one generation's successes and invest them in the next generation.

FEASTING AT THE FAMILY TABLE

When one member of the family brings something to the table, everyone in the family has access to it.

I learned a lot about inheritance once when I went to Tanzania with Jack Taylor, my spiritual father, and a group of leaders. They were learning that inheritance involved things in heaven that God wanted here on earth. They knew they had access to my account. They also realized they had access to Papa Jack's account—the wisdom and revelation from a lifetime of study and experience in the kingdom. They valued what Jack had paid for and tapped into it, and it was beautiful how they started to steward that. We could see how the generation of blessings began to flow.

After that, we began to do some conferences with Papa Jack, myself, and Paul Yadao, my spiritual son—three spiritual generations. The three-generational blessings flowed, and others tapped into them and were transformed. *It was not a matter of what was being taught but of what was being caught.* Today we have people who are living from inheritance in 22 nations and have access to one another's accounts.

How is this possible? When I go out with one of my children, another wants to see the receipt. That's because she knows she will have the same access to whatever I spent on her sister. The family understands what is available. With both Papa God and with others who are stewarding an inheritance, we have access to the things that belong to the family. You realize when you're looking at a receipt that if someone has a breakthrough in the glory realm and you honor that, it can also be yours because you're part of the family. When someone gets a breakthrough into signs, wonders, and miracles, you can tap into that.

We have seen this work again and again as our leaders started to step into nations. They went to India and stepped into some of the same things we were doing in Pakistan because they realized they had the same rights and inheritance. They have changed the atmosphere where they are because they got a vision for their father's dream and started to dream themselves. They are seeing transformation and experiencing blessing. Thousands of people throughout the world have learned the Chair 1 lifestyle. They are living Chair 1 marriages, running Chair 1 businesses, and worshiping and ministering together in Chair 1 churches.

Inheritance is a family term because the kingdom is a family culture. The Bible gives us pictures of Abraham, Isaac, Jacob, and Joseph, or of David and Solomon, to illustrate the father-son dynamics of inheritance. We also see it in non-family relationships like Elijah and Elisha or Moses and Joshua, but these were spiritual fathers and sons. They did not have contracts with each other but were in covenant together. Moses spoke to God as men speak face to face, and Joshua got to listen in, experience the benefits of that intimacy, and enter into the Promised Land. David was a man after God's own heart and fought many battles, and his son got to experience the peace. This is the kingdom way because the blueprint in heaven was of family relationships—the Father, Son, and Spirit. The kingdom culture we are developing here is supposed to look like heaven.

OUR "NOW AND NOT YET" INHERITANCE

When you are at rest and are becoming a resting place for the Dove, an open heaven becomes part of your inheritance. This is very much determined by the way we think whether we are seeing from a Chair 2 or a Chair 1 worldview. Jesus has actually already opened heaven over us for us to walk in. All we have to do is put our Son-glasses on and see the Father's face. Jesus told His followers He was going to prepare a place for them so that "where I am, there you may be also" (John 14:3). Our instinct is to think of that as a promise for after death and to put it in our funeral sermons. It's actually an invitation for right now too though. When you are in the Spirit, you can suddenly go places and do things. You and your family can live under an open heaven, and heaven's resources begin to flow.

I love the story of how Jacob became Israel because there are lessons of both identity and intimacy in it. It especially teaches us about inheritance. Jacob was a wrestler, even from his mother's womb. He outmaneuvered his brother, Esau, for his birthright and his father's blessing. He wanted his inheritance, and he would steal or deceive to get it. Even his name meant deceiver. Yet God saw him through the lenses of his destiny, not his history. As Jacob journeyed to his family's homeland, fleeing his brother's anger, God gave him an open-heaven encounter as he rested on a stone, and Jacob became aware of the Father's presence (Genesis 28:10-22). This is a wonderful picture for us—that resting on the rock leads to an open heaven and revelation of a Father-son relationship. Jacob began to find his identity in that resting place on a solid foundation. It was a glimpse of what was to come for him; he discovered that encounters come from places of rest, not striving. Angels, God's agents of provision, were ascending and descending over him. Jacob called the place Bethel—"house of God"—and God prospered him.

During his time in the east, Jacob was tricked into working an extra seven years for his father-in-law. That's a normal consequence for Chair 2; Jacob had always been a trickster, and you reap what you sow. After he had served the full time for his father-in-law, he took his family and returned to Canaan. He knew he would eventually encounter Esau, who was still probably very angry. On the way, God's angels met him at a site where he camped, and Jacob received word that Esau was coming with 400 men. The night before he knew he would encounter Esau, Jacob had a mysterious wrestling match with God. That may be hard for us to understand, but Jacob had come to a place from Chair 2 where he had done the best a man can do for God. Now God was going to show Jacob what He could do through a man. He moved Jacob to Chair 1 and gave him a new identity.

LIVING FROM INHERITANCE

Surrender is the place of exchange.

Jacob had fought for blessings before, and now he was wrestling for another one. This one would be different. From now on, he would not be living *for* his inheritance; he would be living *from* it. Genesis 32:28 says he wrestled with God and prevailed. How did he win? Not by pinning God but by getting pinned. At the moment he was most vulnerable, he told God he would not let go until God blessed him. He made that claim at a moment of total surrender, when he could do nothing but cling to God Himself. That's when he got his new name: Israel. There is inheritance in that name; it means "one who strives with God" or "triumphant with God," but it also means "prince." It implies royalty. God could entrust him with inheritance.

Now, even if Esau was coming to kill him, Jacob/Israel was at rest. Over the course of his life, he had learned the difference between God's visitation and His habitation—not an encounter-to-encounter relationship but an awareness that God was with him always. He had learned his true identity. He knew who he was, even if his life was in danger. Something else had shifted too; he saw Esau differently: "I have seen your face as though I had seen the face of God" (Genesis 33:10). His perceptions had changed. He was aligned with the family blueprint of seeing God's face. Now he was ready to walk fully in his inheritance, and the inheritance of Abraham and Isaac began to flow through him. The 12 tribes that came from his children became the nation of Israel.

Much later in the New Testament, the writer of Hebrews mentions three things about Jacob: that he blessed the sons of Joseph, he worshiped, and he leaned on his staff (Hebrews 11:21). What does this mean? I believe leaning on his staff represents rest. He had learned how to rest in the Father's house. Second, he built altars and worshiped. You will always see that in sons and daughters of inheritance. Those seeking a blessing may worship God in order to get something, but mature children of inheritance just worship God. And finally, he crossed his arms to bless his grandsons, the sons of his beloved son Joseph. Old and nearly blind, Jacob could still see in the spirit. He blessed the younger before the older. He bypassed the natural because he saw into the supernatural.

Are you a Jacob or an Israel? In the midst of a restless world, in your weariness and fatigue, can you find an unshakeable rock to lay your head on? You'll find an open heaven there. Are you going through a wrestling match with God? *You win by getting pinned; surrender is the place of exchange.* At that moment, you become an Israel. When you go into a hostile world, can you look into their faces and see the face of God? Has the change in your nature caused you to see others by their potential rather than their past? When a restless world meets you, does it see someone who is at rest? A worshiper? A blesser of supernatural blessings?

A generation today has started a wrestling match with God. If you have captured the face of God through intimacy, things are going to change. Your Esaus will embrace you rather than seek to harm you. The Dove resting on you will change the environment around you. Out of your resting, you will receive and reign. Some will have to change their identity and their level of intimacy, but these will be the evidences. Wearing a robe of righteousness, a ring of authority, and sandals of *shalom*, you will walk under an open heaven. You will value your inheritance, steward it, multiply it, and gain authority. That is the invitation for sons and daughters in this season, and if you accept it, the world will change.

WALKING IN INHERITANCE

When you stop focusing on what you don't have and bring what you do have to the Lord, He can multiply it.

Because of my broken neck and back, I became addicted to prescription painkillers. It became necessary for me to enter a treatment center to get off all the medication I had been on for years. The presence had lifted and I needed healing. I also had a problem with financial support because, as a leader of a worldwide mission organization, I couldn't have any income without traveling, speaking, and selling resources. It was like having a multitude of mouths to feed and only a few loaves and fishes. During the time in rehab I lost thousands of dollars in income, and on top of that I had thousands in medical expenses. I was stuck in Chair 2 and didn't know what to do. Crying out to God, He answered me with the question, "What do you have?" I had nothing that I thought would be useful for income, and I couldn't do anything, or so I thought. My Chair 2 perspective kept me focused on what I didn't have. It was time to change chairs and realize what was available from my inheritance.

While I was recovering, I would listen to Mark, a guy with a pleasant voice on the local radio station, and that was soothing. And there was Jerry, who played piano at our church in Florence, Alabama. Then someone gave me a lot of scripture verses for healing, though I couldn't read them very often because I would get migraines. Finally one day it dawned on me; I had a voice, a piano player, and some verses. I invited Mark from the radio to come in and got to know him. Then I asked Jerry if he wanted to participate in a wonderful project. I gave them the scripture verses, and Jerry played while Mark read, and I just sat back in the chair and received while we recorded. I got blessed by all of this. A Chair 1 view says, "Who else can I bless with it now?" We made thousands of copies of the *Healing Stream* CD and sold it for $10, and not only did it make all I needed with an abundance left over—enough to cover my income and my medical bills—480 people in the first year got healed while they listened to it!

Jesus fed 5,000 men plus the women and children who were there by taking the loaves and fishes, blessing them, and multiplying them. The disciples were thinking of how much work it would take to pay for that many meals (Mark 6:37). Jesus did it from a place of rest, and there were 12 baskets of abundance left over. That is a practical example of how to access our inheritance. With God, there is always a way. *"Small" is the new "big" in the kingdom.* With God, one is the new majority. The Chair 2 mindset is always focused on problems, but a Chair 1 mindset is focused on potential. It moves from lack to sufficiency to abundance.

CHAPTER NINE DEVOTIONAL
Children of Inheritance

So often we think of God's blessings as something that He just has available for us, to give freely from His heart of love. This is true; however, let us not forget that He paid dearly – with the life of His only begotten Son – so that we might receive the riches of His glory. We are indeed children of inheritance! Yet, a wise father doesn't give his children their inheritance until they are mature enough to steward it well. We must learn to be stewards by living close to the Father's heart and feasting at His table in the midst of His Kingdom family culture. It's not what is taught, but what is caught – received from the generations in your life – that brings breakthrough. Because when one family member has breakthrough, it is available to all.

FOCUS AREAS

» Now and not yet inheritance – we have a promise for all eternity and a promise for here and now – Jesus made both available.

» Living from inheritance – wanting to receive vs. knowing you have an inheritance.

» Surrender is the place of inheritance – if you are wrestling with God, let Him pin you like Jacob.

» Walking in inheritance – focusing on what you don't have vs. what you do have and allowing God to multiply it.

REFLECTION

With a great deal of vulnerability, I shared the story of learning how to walk in my inheritance while in rehab by focusing on what I did have rather than what I didn't. God truly took the resources He had put in my hands and multiplied them.

Do you have resources in your hands that are not being multiplied because you see problems instead of promise? If so, hallelujah! You have resources from God. Now, ask yourself what you need to do in order to let God use them to the fullest.

CHAPTER TEN
Children of Blessing

THE JOY OF GIVING

We become what Papa has given us.

If I gave you $100, who would be more blessed: you or me? The Bible says I would (Acts 20:35). When we get excited about a gift, it usually isn't because we're excited for the giver who will be blessed for it; it's for the receiver who got an unexpected blessing. Why is that? Because a Chair 2 perspective tends to live from lack while longing for abundance. A Chair 1 worldview lives from abundance.

Jesus and Peter had a tax issue, and Peter didn't have any money to pay it (Matthew 17:24-27). Because Jesus was always in Chair 1, He didn't focus on what was lacking. He told Peter to go catch a fish and find a coin in its mouth, and that would pay for the taxes. Why did Jesus give Peter this peculiar instruction? Because Peter knew how to fish. He wouldn't tell him to go make a healing CD or do a prophetic painting. When He asks us, "What do you have?" it fits in the sphere of what we do and know. Peter's area of expertise was fishing, so that's where Jesus' instructions fit. Peter followed instructions and discovered abundance.

The point I am making is that even when we long to access our inheritance, we still often live with the worldview of an orphan, focused on lack and trying to work toward abundance rather than working from abundance. This is a perception problem, a worldview issue. If you can make that switch, you will not only get more joy from giving than receiving, you will also be able to tap into what you need for what you are called to do. No longer will your decision whether to go on a mission trip be based on whether you see funds available for it. You will see His face and hear His voice, and that's enough. Fear keeps us from aligning for our assignment, but our identity as sons and daughters tells us the Spirit of the Lord is upon us and He has anointed us. Where others have bad news, we have good news. Where others have guilt and shame, we have freedom. We leave behind the orphan mentality and go back to sonship. That's where the Dove comes in, and that's where we start to receive.

THE GREAT "I AM"

After Jesus' resurrection, the disciples were in a room with the door shut. They were still afraid of the mood of the city and the people in power who had crucified Jesus. They were stuck in Chair 2 because they did not yet understand what was going on, even after having been with Jesus for three and a half years. They were where a lot of people are today—needing a breakthrough.

Then Jesus came in. He didn't need to knock on the door. His presence came in and changed the environment. He released *shalom*: "Peace be with you" (John 20:19). From this peace, there came a new provision: He showed them His hands and side (20:20). He showed Himself to be the "I am." All problems would pale in comparison. Anything the disciples needed was in their inheritance. They were afraid? He has perfect love, which casts out fear. Sickness? He heals. Death? He's alive. All issues have to go through the "I Am." We experience His presence, and in His presence we experience peace, and in His peace we experience provision.

Verse 20 says they became glad. To put it another way, they got a new passion. They were suddenly in Chair 1. Their environment had changed, and so had their outlook. In the sinful world we are living in, everything changes with His presence, His peace, and His provision when we no longer look at the problems and the need. Our outlook changes depending on the glasses we are looking through.

When you put on the Son-glasses, He says,

» "I am."

» We say, "You are."

» And then the world sees us and says, "He is!"

Once Jesus got these disciples into alignment, they were ready for their assignment. "As the Father has sent Me, I also send you" (20:21). They had a new purpose to go with their new passion. They had no idea how to do it in Chair 2, so He not only gave them more peace, He gave them new power (20:22). He gave them authority to forgive the sins of others or retain them (20:23) because they were going to represent Him now. He entrusted them with the keys of forgiveness because their view of the world would no longer be the same. They knew the way of the Father - go into the world as a lamb, a lion, or an eagle—whichever is needed for whatever time. You are priests and kings, a royal priesthood.

That is a heavy responsibility, and the Chair 2 church doesn't always handle it well. We prophesy judgment on cities and cultures and watch it come to pass, not because the Father judges them but because we have come into agreement with an enemy who wants to kill, steal, and destroy rather than a God who wants to restore. We need to have the heart of Abraham, who bargained with God to withhold judgment (Genesis 18). The question is not how much darkness is in a place but the lack of light there. *If we really understand our inheritance and know how to access it, we will be able to bring light into dark places rather than condemnation.*

CHAIR 1 VISION

Changing the way we see is a process. When we hear a report of radicals burning down Christian homes and businesses, or suicide bombers devastating a marketplace full of innocent people, it is difficult not to get angry. I used to look at these situations and think harsh judgments about them. I still feel that they are horrific, but the difference now is that I see an invitation to dream with God. When I see an enemy that comes to kill, steal, and destroy, I turn my focus to the One who comes to give abundant life. In the past, I didn't know how to be a change agent. I was overwhelmed with the darkness because I could see no way to make a difference. *When you love, you don't ask God for judgment; you ask Him for solutions.*

In this journey of learning the different worldviews, I began to understand that *you only have authority over what you love.* If you don't love your city or country, you won't get authority over it. When you get God's solutions, you want to be part of the solution. When I began to think in this way, I found myself praying differently about these horrific situations in the world. "Father, do You see the destruction of those terrorists? Whatever they deserve, place that on me because I'm Your priest. I represent these people to You. Where there is sickness and disease, I represent healing and life. I am an ambassador of reconciliation." The Father's heart in you begins a ministry of reconciliation in you. You step into the equation to become a history maker and world changer. Many of us pray from Chair 2, asking God to do what He has called us to do. Nothing is wrong with prayer meetings, but if they become a substitute for our assignment, they are disobedience.

When Abraham was negotiating with God to spare Sodom and Gomorrah, God wasn't the one who stopped. Abraham asked him to withhold judgment first for the sake of 50 people and got all the way down to 10, then didn't go any lower. But what if he had? What if there was only one left? Eventually there was, and God placed the sin of us all on His shoulders at the cross. He took sickness and disease on Himself so that by His stripes, we are healed (Isaiah 53:5). He took the punishment of us all. And then He called us to follow in His footsteps—to take up our cross and follow Him. We can; we are already righteous in the Father's eyes, already loved as much as we will ever be. Absorbing the sins of others is not going to lessen our status before the Father. That's what priests do. *We never go in to attack the people; we attack the enemy behind the people.*

As I began to see Muslims differently, God opened doors to make a difference in their culture. It didn't matter to Him if the desire to bring peace looked impossible. He specializes in impossible. We went in and loved on the family. Just recently we sent a check to help pay for the hospital and funeral expenses of victims of a suicide bombing. Then we went in to bring restoration. We rented a cricket stadium, and God did 3,000 creative miracles there, healed 30,000 people, and saved 87,200. That turned the enemy's strategy on its head. You overcome evil with good, not with judgment.

If the enemy knows that every time he attacks there will be a tsunami of love, the world will be changed.

Jesus said it was actually better for Him to go away than to remain (John 16:7) because that meant His presence could be everywhere rather than in one place. It is a very real presence. From that presence, we have peace; and from that peace, we have provision. From that place, we get new passion and new power, we are sent on assignment with a new program and purpose, and we begin to see from a new paradigm. The Father sent Jesus, and Jesus sent us in the same way He had been sent. Now our view of the world has everything to do with how He will treat it. When we know He is good, we will show the kindness that leads to repentance. *We re-present on earth what's in heaven.*

INHERITANCE BRINGS ACCESS

Do you see now how our inheritance is much more than getting blessings from the Father's storehouse? How it involves much more than claiming what we think He has promised without living from the covenant? Our Son-glasses are our inheritance. How we see determines what we experience and what the world around us experiences in us. *Through our access to our inheritance, the world can have access to the Father.* That is at least some of what Paul means in Colossians 1:27 when he writes about "Christ in you, the hope of glory." Our lives reveal to those in Chair 3—those who have no idea how to access heaven— what heaven is like. In us, they can encounter Jesus. So too can those in Chair 2. Even though they know Him and believe in heaven, they don't think heaven is available while we are on earth. Our union with the Father, Son, and Spirit demonstrates the heavenly blueprint here and now.

The world longs for a revelation of the sons and daughters of God (Romans 8:19). Chairs 2 and 3, even with different belief systems, are in one way or another trying to belong. Chair 2 tries to belong to God, Chair 3 to the world. They believe they have to behave in order to belong. But Chair 1 believers know we belong, therefore we behave like sons and daughters. We demonstrate to the world what it's like to belong in Papa's house. *We become the revelation the world is looking for.* We learn how to steward and access our inheritance. With the Son, we inherit the world.

CHAPTER TEN DEVOTIONAL
Children of Blessing

In the gospel of Matthew, chapter 17, we find the story of the coin in the fish's mouth. The disciples are in need of money to pay taxes. Without Son-glasses, they see lack. Jesus, however, sees abundance. He knows that God will supply every need according to His riches in glory. We are sons and daughters of Papa God and everything the Father has is available to us when we receive the sonship of Jesus. These resources are not limited to physical things such as a coin in a fish's mouth. They include the *shalom* of God – the immeasurable peace His presence brings to us – along with love, authority, wisdom, and power. He sends us into the world as either a lamb, a lion or an eagle, depending on the circumstance. We are continually equipped from that place close to the heart of God.

FOCUS AREAS

»   Putting on the Son-glasses – "I am." "You are." "He is!"

»   Chair 1 vision – dream with God even in our darkest moments.

»   Overcome evil with good – attack the enemy behind the people, not the people.

REFLECTION QUESTIONS

1. Think of a time when you were in the midst of a dark moment in your life. Were you operating from Chair 1 or Chair 2? If your answer was Chair 1, make a note of how you were able to be in Chair 1 and keep it handy for future reference. If your answer was Chair 2, think about how you could have moved from Chair 2 to Chair 1 and be determined to use this strategy the next time you are facing difficult circumstances.

2. How do you understand the concept that we should attack the enemy behind the people and not the people themselves? How would this shift in strategy change the outcome?

3. Can you think of anyone, either in history or your own life, who dreamed with God in the midst of their darkest moments? What do you think gave them the ability to do this?

CHAPTER ELEVEN
The Access Point

HANDLING DRY SEASONS

I went through a barren season in 2000, and in the middle of it, I visited a church in Illinois where I met a wealthy lawyer who had bought up many big farms. He had actually been brought up on a farm, then became a business lawyer and rose to second position in a very large law firm. As we were driving through thousands of acres of farmland, I said, "Kent, it looks like you're losing the corn, the soybeans, everything. You're losing the harvest."

"Leif, let me tell you a story," he said. "It looked like we were going to lose the corn because we had a dry season. For months, it looked like the sun was just beating down on the corn without any relief. We didn't realize that in desperation, the roots of the corn kept going deeper and deeper. Then we had a downpour of rain, and there was so much of it we thought that was going to destroy the corn because it would not be able to absorb all the water. Instead, what happened was the roots had gone deep because of the dry season, and when the rain soaked into the ground, they were deep and strong enough to absorb more than ever and get all the nutrients they need. We're going to have the best harvest ever."

In the driest season of my life, when everything was drying up financially, spiritually, practically, relationally, and physically, I learned how to walk with God. I learned that I had a robe, a ring, and sandals. Then, after my roots had grown deep, a downpour came. Sometimes you learn intimacy in the wilderness. The wilderness can be a preparation for inheritance. But how do you handle those dry seasons?

I was at a conference at a church at Central Baptist Church (Abba's House) in Hixson, Tennessee, with a couple of friends. I had been in this dry season and was hungry and thirsty for more. This church had fresh bread; they had brought in some great speakers. My friends and I knew it would be a full house, but we saw some empty seats up front and went to see if we could get them. An usher quickly put us in our proper place; those seats were reserved for VIPs. In an earlier time, it would have been humiliating to walk all the way to the front like that and then be turned away to walk all the way back with everyone watching. But how can you humiliate someone who has already been humbled? I had just gone through a very humbling season, so I wasn't bothered. I walked back with my friends and found a place underneath the balcony.

No one there knew who I was, but my Father did because I had a robe, a ring, and some sandals. We had had a party, a covenantal meal, when I came back into the Father's house. He slaughtered a calf for me and celebrated. He spent a long time teaching me just to be His son—not to value Him for what He could do for me, but to value Him for Him. I had spent much of my life trusting in the things in His estate rather than actually trusting in Him. As I was sitting underneath the balcony, I was sure no one was going to notice me. I had some Chair 2 thoughts, but I reminded myself, "Wow, Papa, I'm a son, and because I'm a son, all that You have is mine. It doesn't matter if anyone else sees me. You do. It doesn't matter what anyone else thinks of me because I know what You think of me. I know Your acceptance and can feel Your love. I know who I am and whose I am. I have my identity and my intimacy with You, and that's enough."

I just sat there thinking about my inheritance, being amazed at all the things that belong to my Father, thankful that He had been showing me maturity and teaching me to go from a son of blessing to a son of inheritance. If He had withheld inheritance at times, it was because it would harm me. I could trust Him to give it to me when it would help me bring blessings to generations to come. I sat there in a Chair 1 attitude, overwhelmed, secure in love, value, and purpose.

Charles Carrin, a spiritual father who had acknowledged me as a son was speaking that day. One of the other speakers was Bishop Joseph Garlington, who preached a message I have never forgotten: Quantum Worship. In the middle of his message, he said, "There's a Leif Hetland here. You are supposed to pray for me and my wife, Barbara." When the message was over, it felt like everyone in the room was about to go forward, but Bishop Garlington called me forward while everyone else watched and wondered, "Who is this guy?"

When I went up there and prayed, we all hit the floor. Later on, the usher who had shown us to the back of the auditorium told me he wanted me to pray for people up front. The next day, Dr. Ron Phillips asked, "What can we do for you, son? Who are you?" I didn't have any resources, but a group of people there gave me a couple of laptops and some support, and I went to Pakistan and was able to be a blessing there. It started a journey with the Father that took me away from the perspective that there are only so many pieces in the pizza to the perspective that my Father owns the whole bakery. There is abundance in His house. He was teaching me to trust Him in the small things. When I didn't need His blessing to tell me who I was, I got His blessing to help me do what He called me to do. *When you don't need God's favor to feel validated as a son or daughter, that's when you'll get it because He knows He can trust you.*

SONSHIP

A few weeks later, Randy Clark called from Brazil and said, "Somebody just told me about you." Randy had prayed for me six years earlier, but did not remember me out of the many he had prayed for. He had heard about me after I had been called out at the conference in Tennessee. God was beginning to stir things up. It would still be a few more years before I finished the transition from a son of blessing to a son of inheritance. In 2005, I shifted from what some people call the "dark night of the soul" to what I call being a molting eagle. I had been managing several "ships"—apostleship, leadership, stewardship, relationships, friendships—and all of my ships got shipwrecked. I was left with one: sonship - and it's the most beautiful ship in the world.

When I came up from that place of shipwreck, I didn't need anything any longer. I didn't value God only for what I could get out of Him. I didn't value Papa Jack—Jack Taylor, my spiritual father— for what he did for me. I just woke up in the morning and valued being a son to God and to Papa Jack. I didn't value them for what they could do for me but for who they were to me. In my mind, there was no pressure on either of them to do anything for me for the rest of my life. I was content to be a son. In that season, I had become a son of inheritance. The Father said, "Ask of Me, and I will give You the nations for Your inheritance, and the ends of the earth for Your possession" (Psalm 2:8). *When you don't need anything, you can be entrusted with everything.*

STEWARDING WITH WISDOM

The nations are gifts of inheritance for those who will steward and care for them.

In Psalm 2, God says, "You are My Son, today I have begotten You" (2:7). Sons and daughters can ask for the nations, because we are co-heirs with Him. From my Chair 2 perspective, I had always looked at the nations as problems to solve. Now in Chair 1, they became promises. How do we receive God's promises? We have to steward what we have been given, and it is important in our stewardship to have wisdom, which is thinking like God thinks. *Wisdom is always connected to inheritance.* Wisdom is knowing what to do with knowledge. It is a gift from the Father.

Around the world today we are seeing revival fire burning in 22 nations through Global Mission Awareness. This fire is burning brightly without burning out because we have sons and daughters of inheritance who know how to steward nations. Some are stewarding businesses, others ministries. In every case, it begins with the individual coming home to the Father, then marriages and businesses and relationships coming home to the Father, getting into Chair 1, and understanding identity and intimacy. They capture the Father's heart and His ears, growing in wisdom and favor with God and man. Then they move from being sons and daughters of blessing to sons and daughters of inheritance. They take responsibility for the estate on earth and learn how to steward it with the resources of heaven. When we steward one talent well the Father will give us more—not as a reward for performance but as a natural increase in capacity.

INTO THE PROMISED LAND

When we see things as a Son, and envision what the Father is seeing, access opens up and inheritance begins to flow.

Sons and daughters of the Father receive the Promised Land from within intimate relationship. We learn how to live not *for* victory but *from* victory. The land has already been given to us, but receiving it is still a process. We must learn how to come into position. We grow in maturity in order to take responsibility for our inheritance. We can inherit cities and nations, but we still have to learn how to make it through the places of wilderness.

God gives us the best seed, but if it does not fall into the right soil, it will not work. The right soil is a face-to-face relationship with God from Chair 1. When the soil is the environment of heaven the seeds of heaven will grow in it. When Jesus died on the cross and the veil between God and man, between heaven and earth, ripped open, we had an open heaven. Most of us today still have a closed heaven between our ears. Our Bethel—our house of God—is still open, but we have to know how to see it. We have to know how to access the inheritance.

When I go into Pakistan, everything in the natural often appears to be shut. Since I don't live from the natural anymore I know that "one is the new majority" and "small is the new big." I know that one son or daughter with the Dove, seated in heavenly places with the Son and in intimate fellowship with the Father, can change the environment. Canaan had already been promised to Israel when Joshua led them into it, but it still took 31 years to occupy. Inheritance rarely falls into our laps. There is often a fight and a process.

Jesus already paid for everything. He took our sin, guilt, and shame on Himself at the cross—that's the gospel of salvation—but He did much more. He also opened up a heaven full of resources for every son and daughter of the kingdom. Jesus inherited everything (Hebrews 1:2), and we are co-heirs with Him (Romans 8:17). We can write checks on that account as mature sons and daughters who know how to steward what we have been given. *The master key to the family account is sonship.* The identity and intimacy we find in our relationship with the Father give us access to everything He has. They open up all the estate's rooms and all the family accounts.

Some of us have been sitting in Chair 2 waiting for the Father while He has been home waiting for us. He wants to move His children, both the rebellious and the religious, from Chair 2 to Chair 1. He wants us to come home so we can receive the inheritance He has prepared for us and then steward and invest that inheritance in the right way. He wants us to use what we have been given to go after all that has been lost so that what is in heaven can be manifested here on earth. God doesn't want us to consume our inheritance for ourselves but to invest it in restoration. It is meant for increase—for the kingdom to be built on the foundations that have already been given.

CHAPTER ELEVEN DEVOTIONAL
The Access Point

In this chapter we find the story of crops that were able to withstand a severe dry season because they grew deep roots during the drought so that when the rains came, they had the depth needed to benefit from the deluge. This is a picture of God's desire for us – to sink our roots deep into the soil of His heart so that we can withstand the dry seasons. When we have learned how to come into the place of rest with God, we don't need His favor to feel validated. We live from favor, not for it. We get His blessings to help us do what He has called us to do, rather than to tell us our identity. In this secure place we are able to withstand the dark night of the soul. When you don't need anything, you can be entrusted with everything.

FOCUS AREAS

» The Identity Thief – the age-old lie that began in the Garden.

» The Truth Deficiency – identity confusion violates the Kingdom family culture and leads to an orphan spirit.

» Recognizing Lucifer's Strategy – to keep us from intimacy with God.

REFLECTIONS

When we see with heaven's eyes, we see promises instead of problems. Think of something in your life that you see as a problem, and then make your way over to Chair 1 and see it as a promise. If you are having difficulty changing your glasses or perspective, ask Holy Spirit to show you how He sees the situation.

Using the example of Joshua leading Israel into the Promised Land and how it took 31 years, reflect on the length of time it is taking you to get to God's promised land. Are you experiencing a process; a fight to get to where you are destined to be? What is God doing along the way to help you?

To envision what the Father is seeing is to see things as a son or daughter of the King. From this position access begins to open up and inheritance begins to flow. What things in your life are you envisioning in the same way that God does?

Part Three Summary Reflection:
INHERITANCE

What Do I Have?

Chapter 8 talks about the maturity and wisdom necessary for stewarding our inheritance. God is looking for mature sons and daughters who can deal with the gifts and blessings He gives us. Then, when we are ready, He will entrust us with heaven's riches. He will put His ring of understanding and authority on your finger, the yoke of sonship on your shoulders, and clad your feet with the shoes of peace. This is your inheritance as a royal priest who represents the environment of heaven. Chapter 9 focuses on how we are to receive from the generations in our life by feasting at God's table in the midst of His Kingdom family culture. This is where breakthrough happens, and that breakthrough is available to every member of the family. Chapter 10 reminds us that we are blessed children of the Father who supplies our every need, both physical and spiritual, according to His riches in glory in Christ Jesus! Hallelujah! Chapter 11 focuses on how we endure dry seasons on the way to our destiny. In the place of intimacy, close to the heart of God, our roots grow deep and strong, equipping us to withstand times of drought as we walk out God's calling on our life.

ACTIVATION

» All of us experience seasons when it seems like everything is coming against the destiny God has for us. We feel like we should have made it to the Promised Land long ago and yet we are still struggling. When you are in the midst of a dry season it's easy to forget the times of abundance with the Father. Why is it that dry seasons tend to make us take off our Songlasses? Take a few minutes and make a timeline of your journey to your destiny. Indicate the times of abundance and the dry seasons. Think about how you stewarded your seasons of abundance and how you navigated the dry seasons. Make note of those Chair 1 times when you were able to receive as a beloved son or daughter, and those times when you wandered over into Chair 2 and lost sight of who you are and who God is. Keep your timeline handy, referring to it when necessary, and adding to it as you go.

PART FOUR
DESTINY

What Am I Called to Do?

"'I know the plans I have for you,' declares the Lord, 'plans to prosper you and not to harm you, plans to give you hope and a future'" (Jeremiah 29:11 NIV). I keep this verse in the front of my notebook because it is very much a focus of mine. It only makes sense in the context of my identity as a son, my intimacy with the Father, and the inheritance I am stewarding and multiplying. I know that everything purchased on the cross was not given to me just so I could get to heaven but so heaven could get into me and the world around me. I know I was created with a destiny.

Destiny is the fourth part of this book. The section on identity answered the question, "Who am I?" The chapters on intimacy answered the question, "Where am I in my walk with the Lord?" The part on inheritance answered the question, "What do I have?" Now we are going to see, "What am I called to do?" because you do have a calling. Even before you were in your mother's womb (Jeremiah 1:5)—and even before the foundation of the world (Ephesians 1:4)—you had a divine destiny.

CHAPTER TWELVE
Papa's Family

I was at a meeting of denomination leaders in the Philippines that included both evangelical and charismatic streams. I was there to speak on kingdom alignment. One of the men was a well-respected leader, a little imposing but very influential, and I was impressed with how everyone treated him and talked about him. In his 70s at the time, he had once been the youngest president of a major bank in the Philippines. He had gotten saved years ago, and he had done a lot to advance the church in his country, sponsoring major events and bringing in big-time speakers. He was a world-changer in this part of the world, but I didn't know how to connect with his heart. I felt it might be a challenge.

One night our group was sitting in a restaurant, and this man sat at a nearby table. I was looking at him when I had a Chair 1 encounter—I could see him based on his destiny, almost like this older man was a son of mine. Though he was sitting at another table, our eyes met, and something hit him. The people sitting around us can testify that it felt like a wave came into the restaurant. It was a baptism of love that transformed everything in his life.

From that moment on, we started to hang out and became very close friends. People noticed the change in him, and they could see the ripple effect it had in his family. He had grown up in that very performance-oriented emphasis that is sometimes common to Asian culture, but now he got comfortable with receiving and expressing love. Everywhere he went, all around the world, environments around him began to change. He carried something more than leadership; he carried a family culture.

When your inner environment changes, you start to become an environment changer. You live and move in the power and wisdom of love. You see people not for the way they are but the way they are going to be. Where others see a Saul, you see a Paul. You not only begin to step into your destiny. You help others step into theirs.

THE FAMILY CULTURE

What was God's purpose from the beginning? If you recall our discussion of creation and Eden, we saw that the Father, Son, and Spirit wanted to make man "in our image." The destiny of the kingdom family was to create on earth the kind of love, honor, and unity that there is in heaven. After six days of creation, God breathed into dust and made a man who saw His face, heard His voice, felt His love, experienced His presence, and lived in His pleasure.

One of the key signs of the resting place was that God worked for six days and rested on the seventh. Since He made human beings on the sixth day, humanity's first day of existence was a day of rest. God is saying something profound in this story: *our starting point is a place of rest*. It's something of a paradox, but we are always meant to work from rest. The Chair 2 tendency is to rest from work. Ours is the opposite. We work from rest. Rest is connected to anything we are created to do. We are not designed to struggle with our identity, our intimacy, or our inheritance. We are simply to receive from the Father. Jesus said, "Freely you have received; freely give" (Matthew 10:8). Everything we do is going to come from Him, go through us, and go back to Him. *Our destiny depends on our rest.*

We saw that both Adam and Eve had an encounter with God before being brought together, and that God blessed them. It takes the blessing of a father to unlock the destiny in sons and daughters. God blessed them to be, not to do. Their doing was always to come out of their being.

> *It isn't what we do that makes us who we are,*
> *but who we are that determines what we do.*

In Chair 1, Adam and Eve were to "be fruitful." It's the same way in the Spirit: we are to be love, to be joy, to be peace. As He is, so are we in this world (1 John 4:17). We don't even have to focus on what we're doing. If we are who we are, what we do will flow from our identity. *What we become, we multiply, and what we multiply, we get authority over.* That was the Father's blessing: be fruitful, multiply, take dominion, and I will give you authority. *God gave them the assignment of taking what the Father, Son, and Spirit had in heaven and filling the whole earth with the same love, unity, glory, honor, peace, and joy.* This is a family on a mission.

Adam and Eve's destiny started well in a garden. There was no fear, insecurity, or guilt. The Father's dream was becoming a reality. He had a family on earth that looked like heaven. We know it didn't end up that way, of course, and yet God already had a plan for restoration before the foundation of the world. They lost their destiny. They moved into the wrong chair and began a journey to figure out who they were and whose they were. Their struggle is the same one most of the world is experiencing today in Chair 2 or 3 – living outside the culture of God. God's goal is to spread the culture of His family across the earth.

» **Chair 2** works to evangelize the world, not from a place of rest or an environment of family. They focus on getting people saved so they can go to heaven.

» **Chair 1** wants to see people adopted into the family so they can get heaven into them.

STRATEGIC PREPARATION

If God has a calling and destiny for each of us, as His Word says, then each of us are part of His dream. He wrapped your body around something He had in His mind; clearly, He cares about what we do. He is intensely interested in His sons and daughters succeeding. It is of the highest importance to know who we are and whose we are—to settle our identity and intimacy. From that place comes our inheritance. When we know these things, we go out and do, not from occasional visitations from the Lord but from a place of habitation. Everything we do comes out of relationship.

We see this dynamic in the lives of many Bible characters. God took His time with the key people in Scripture because they had to learn who they were and who He was before they did what He called them to do. Abram grew in faith to become Abraham, the father of nations. Moses was supposed to be a deliverer of three million slaves to take them from Egypt to the Promised Land—and he did, but only after 40 years of preparation in Egypt and 40 years of isolation in Midian. David was destined for the throne of Israel, but only after years of finding his identity and intimacy on the run in the wilderness and in caves and the crisis of battle. *The enemy doesn't attack copies; he goes for the original.* If you were to tell me where the devil has attacked you the most, I would probably be able to tell you where your destiny is, because the serpent often bites you where you have the greatest authority.

Wherever you are connected with destiny is where Satan has bitten. When you get to the other side of that experience, you will find authority there.

I was called to be an ambassador of love. That is why many of my attacks have come in the area of fear. My years of preparation have involved a lot of experience in love casting out fear (1 John 4:18). Years of preparation are not easy, but they are strategic. The Father uses them to cultivate the identity and relationship from which your inheritance and destiny flow. Moses is a good example of this.[1] At the time he was born, the devil was picking up on the idea that Israel's destiny was about to unfold. There had been a prophecy of 400 years in slavery for God's people (Genesis 15:13), and the time for a deliverer was approaching. Moses was floated down the Nile in a basket and survived an attempt to wipe out a generation of Hebrew baby boys. He grew up in the world system—Chair 3—knowing the culture, language, economy, and philosophy of Egypt. He knew how Pharaoh thought. He lived in Egypt for 40 years, and from all appearances, he was ready for his destiny as a deliverer. He even made an attempt to protect the people of Israel by killing an abusive Egyptian, but instead of becoming a deliverer he became an exile. *It took 40 years to get Moses out of Egypt, and another 40 years to get Egypt out of Moses.* He seemed to move from being qualified to being disqualified. And then God was ready.

---

1 Jack Taylor, who has been a spiritual father to me, got me interested in Moses (and is somewhat of a Moses himself), so I've studied Moses' life quite a bit.

You will see this pattern often in people's lives. Right now, God is setting many people free from addiction through people who were once addicted and then set free. You have authority in the areas where the devil once attacked you. Never underestimate the importance of the process toward your destiny. When you walk through incredible difficulties or long wildernesses to gain freedom, you gain authority. Moses was one of those people.

When God finally encountered Moses at a burning bush (see Exodus 3-4), Moses needed to be reoriented to the assignment he had long forgotten. "When people ask who has sent me, what should I say?" he asked.

"Tell them 'I am,'" said God.

Not only was this confusing grammar; it isn't very specific. But God's message to His sons and daughters is that He is everything we need. *He says, "I am your healer, deliverer, authority, presence, peace, strength, sufficiency, abundance, destiny, everything."* In any situation, we need to be able to look to God and say, "You are." Whatever the need is, the answer is Him. Then the people around us will see and begin to say, "He is. He's a good God, a peaceful God, a powerful God," and on and on.

Moses still didn't see it. He felt completely insufficient. So God asked him, "What is that in your hand?"

"A rod," Moses answered. It was his identity, his inheritance as a shepherd. It represented what he did—his provision and protection.

God was about to give him a new identity. "Lay it down."

Many of us would argue at this point. God often steps into our journey toward our destiny and redefines it. Jesus did that with His disciples. They were busy fishing—their identity—and He told them to leave their nets so He could make them fishers of men.

When Moses laid down the rod of his identity, it became a serpent. There was a poisonous nature in the thing Moses held as his security. We rarely recognize this when God tests our destiny. What is in our hands? Is it His ministry or ministry with a "hiss"? Even in the very things He gives us, if they become something other than His, they can have a hiss to them and be as dangerous as a serpent. When Moses laid down his rod, the nature of the world left it. The poison was gone. God said, "Now I want you to pick it back up."

Now Moses was in Chair 1. It was God's rod in the hands of God's man. Moses was holding God's ability, power, authority, presence, and peace—everything he needed to fulfill his destiny. Moses' journey very often parallels our journey. We have to see God differently, see ourselves differently, and see whatever is in our hands differently. Is it a rod? It's God's. Is it ability or wisdom or power? It's God's.

"I'VE GOT YOU"

Moses started the journey of delivering God's people, and it wasn't always easy. He often went back to a perspective from the wrong chair, just as you and I do in our journey. The problems begin to look bigger than God. Moses often presented his Chair 2 perspective to

God: "Lord, we have a problem. I'm trying to lead these three million people from Chair 3 to the resting place of Chair 1, and they are so restless. They want to go back again!"

"Excuse Me," the Lord would answer. "What exactly was the problem?"

"I just told you."

"What do you have in your hand? What have I given you?"

"Oh yeah. I've got Your wisdom, Your authority, Your peace, Your presence. I've got You."

We can see this play out again and again. Moses was caught between the Red Sea in front of him and Egypt's army behind him. Again the question was "what did he have in his hand," because *with a vision there is always provision.* When God is calling you to do something, He is obligated to fulfill it. It's His responsibility. You will have to maintain your sense of identity because the enemy is always trying to move you away from knowing that you are a son or daughter of a good, good Father. He wants to disrupt your intimacy so you can no longer hear God's voice, see His face, feel His feelings, experience His presence, and know His pleasure. His strategy is to take your eyes off what is available to you and turn them to what seems not to be available. He wants you to focus on lack rather than on the inheritance you have in Chair 1. That very often works; millions of believers forget that they have everything they need to fulfill everything God has called them to do and be when it's right in their hands.

CARRIERS OF HIS GLORY

What is already in our hands? We are sons and daughters of the Father, and the Dove rests upon us. We are called to be carriers of His habitation—to live from heaven toward earth rather than from earth toward heaven. That's a completely different mindset. Most believers are living from earth trying to pull heaven's resources into their lives. We are already in the Father's house wearing His robe, His ring, and His sandals. We have access to heaven's resources and can carry them from heaven into earth. That makes us culture changers. The Son carries His government and His peace upon His shoulders (Isaiah 9:6-7), and we are carriers of the Son. The increase of His government will never end. He is called Mighty God, Everlasting Father, Prince of Peace. That means we rule and reign with Him as kings and priests. We carry a kingdom culture and a family culture—a covenant of love and honor—into the world. It shapes not only what our churches look like but also our marriages, families, businesses, and other areas of involvement.

How does this play out? How do we honor people we disagree with? What does it look like to love God, ourselves, and others from that paradigm? *Everything flows from the Father-Son relationship we see in Jesus.* We also see examples of this inheritance and mission in Moses and Joshua, David and Solomon, and Elijah and Elisha. We are not on a mission of theology or methodology. *We are on a family mission to bring the culture of heaven's family into the world.*

A TRAINING-FOR-REIGNING PROGRAM

God has us in a school where destiny is being tested;
where learning begins in the natural.

We are called to be people of destiny, but many people never recognize theirs. I've noticed four destiny-killers in my life: disappointments, discouragement, distractions, and delays—I call them the four Ds. Any one of these can undermine the destiny we have been given, but they also work in powerful combinations to divert us from fulfilling our true purpose. The destiny of both David and Saul was to be a king, but only one of them fulfilled his destiny. Saul became a king but had his kingdom taken from him because he was not faithful. He was a man after man's own heart, while David was a man after God's own heart. David was faithful in the natural—with his harp, with his sling, in his friendships, in his responsibilities, and in his Bethlehem season. *Faithfulness in the natural realm correlates to faithfulness in the spiritual realm.*

Many believers want to move into the supernatural and change the world. We're in the middle of a training-for-reigning program, but our identity as sons and daughters of the Father needs to include faithfulness in our natural identity too. It took 30 years of preparation before the destiny over Jesus' life was birthed into a three-and-a-half year ministry that changed the world. He learned how to be a faithful son in the natural until the supernatural came in. Then the Father opened heaven over Him and the Dove came down. David was a faithful son to Jesse, his father. He was a shepherd who took care of his father's business. He also knew he was a worshiper and a warrior, a priest and a king. Others had their own dreams, but David had a vision for his father's dream, and that upgraded him into the destiny God had given him.

We are not fulfilling our destiny because we are not living from a place of rest in our identity, intimacy, and inheritance. God is raising up world-changers, giant-slayers, and history-makers who will go through this training-for-reigning program and not shrink back from it. David was willing to take care of his father's business even when a bear or lion came against his father's sheep. No one was going to snatch those sheep away from the family's estate. David knew his responsibility in the natural and his responsibility in the supernatural were connected. David wasn't always in Chair 1. He didn't always have the right perspective during his season in the wilderness. He learned how to get out of Chair 2 and back into Chair 1, as we see in many of his psalms. He often cried out with a focus on his problem, but ended them with a focus on God. During David's years of exile from King Saul, who was trying to hunt him down and kill him, he took refuge in the cave of Adullam. "Everyone who was in distress, everyone who was in debt, and everyone who was discontented gathered to him. So he became captain over them. Now there were about four hundred men with him" (1 Samuel 22:1-2). In the cave David learned how to create a culture to sustain what God had called him to be. He was called to be a king, but if he was going to conquer a kingdom, not just one tribe, he needed to take these people on the margins, create a synergy among them, and develop a covenant relationship. David went from Adullam where everybody was in it for themselves—Chair 2—and came to Hebron, where he reigned for seven years after he became king, before Jerusalem was conquered and made the capital. In Hebron, he developed a new culture that was going to change the old culture. It was a kingdom culture, a family culture that was part of his destiny. That foundation was eventually given to his son Solomon, who took it and established *shalom*. David paid a price. He was at war so his son Solomon could inherit a kingdom. The Bible says there was rest on all sides, with no adversary and no evil threats.

Many people never pass that test; they never come out of the cave or stop seeing it as a problem. David was able to turn his cave into a palace. He could see himself as royalty before he ever sat on a throne because he had learned to see himself as God saw him. That identity began to pull from heaven's resources. David's destiny was not just to kill one giant; it was to raise up an army of giant slayers. It was not just to worship at a temple; it was to create a culture of worshipers. David's destiny was bigger than David and yours is bigger than you.

CHAPTER TWELVE DEVOTIONAL
Papa's Family

You are part of God's family, on a mission. In fact, He designed you for family, and His heart's desire is for you to help spread the culture of His family across the whole earth. Everything you need for this mission can be accessed from Chair 1. When you move out of chair 1, you are in danger of losing your identity and hence your destiny. Your heavenly Father has provided you with Chair 1 access because He knows that destiny can be years in the making. If you stay close to Him, He will prepare you by cultivating the soil of your heart and mind so that your inheritance can take root and flourish. We are made to be carriers of His glory, living from heaven toward earth in God's training-for-reigning program. He is looking for faithful sons and daughters who will allow themselves to go through the necessary equipping to become royalty.

FOCUS AREAS

» Strategic Preparation – where the serpent has bitten you is often the area where you have the greatest authority.

» Rod-ology – what's in your hands? Is it His ministry or ministry with a hiss?

» Training-for-Reigning Program – faithfulness in the natural realm correlates to faithfulness in the spiritual realm.

REFLECTION QUESTIONS

Most organizations today have some sort of mission statement crafted within the family culture of the organization. As believers, we too should have a mission statement. If you don't have one, it's time to sit down with the Father and go about the important work of defining what He has set before you within the larger context of our Kingdom family mission, which is to spread the culture of His family across the earth. As you begin to craft your mission statement, ask Holy Spirit to lead you to scripture that supports your partnership with God. Here are a few questions to get you started. Ask yourself,

1. Where do I fit into this larger mission?

2. What gifts and talents has the Father given me to steward?

3. Am I accessing all the resources made available to me in Christ Jesus?

CHAPTER THIRTEEN
Destiny

GOD'S DREAM AND HOLY SPIRIT'S VISION

One of my hobbies is looking at gravestones. My wife is fascinated with the names and the dates, but I get tears in my eyes thinking about the buried dreams—the songs that were never written, the stories that have never been told, the visions that were never realized. I wonder how many lived full lives but died empty. I know there are plenty of fulfilled dreams represented there too, but I can't help thinking about the ones that never were. What solutions to the world's problems went into those graves? What would poverty or disease look like if the people who dreamed about solutions lived long enough to bring them about? Every life had potential that was not yet reached.

I want to make sure at the end of my life that my dreams and destiny are not left undone.

I told you a little bit of my story in the last section, but here's some more of my background. My mother didn't know she was carrying me in her womb for a time in 1965, but I believe the enemy knew an ambassador of love was about to be born and a destiny was about to be fulfilled. A potential father of the next missionary movement was developing. My mom found out she was pregnant during a surgery, and from then on she was constantly worried what might happen to the child she was carrying. As a result, I was born into fear. That's a great way to become an apostle of love, by the way, because perfect love casts out fear (1 John 4:18). I can see times in my life when the enemy tried to attack. He went after my purity when I was 12. He went after my destiny by lying to me, and I became a prodigal son and eventually a suicidal 18-year-old. Yet God saw me by my destiny, not my history. He saw me as a world-changer, a history-maker, a beloved son. It was an incredible experience when I first got my robe and then got my ring and started fulfilling my destiny.

It has been a long journey. I began to get a glimpse of it when Randy Clark prayed for me June 6, 1995. In the years since, there have been battles because the enemy is always nervous at the prospect of us stepping into our destiny. This should be no surprise; anyone in history who has made a difference has had dreams—because dreams and destiny often go together—and gone through wildernesses, delays, detours, and struggles. God had a dream and Jesus had a vision. Then Jesus had a dream and the Holy Spirit had a vision. Now the Holy

Spirit has a dream and you and I have a vision. What is it? That the Father wants His family back.

If you were to ask why I, Leif Hetland, was born, my answer would be very simple. I want every single person in the world to experience a God who looks like Jesus and loves like Jesus. That's my destiny and it is your destiny too. Your destiny will connect with that vision, even though it may look very different in the way it manifests, because that is God's dream and the Holy Spirit's vision for the world.

What does that look like for me? How do I show the world a God who looks like Jesus? I can see how every place the enemy has tried to take me out has been connected to this destiny. I have a healing ministry, but the enemy has gone after it and I've had numerous health issues and surgeries. My destiny is connected to raising up a family. So where have I been tested? In family—in creating a family culture that can change the culture. This is how it works for all of us. Anytime you find a reliable product on the market, it's because it has been tested numerous times. David passed his tests. Jesus passed his tests. You and I . . . we have everything we need to pass our tests. God wants us to be a full representation of Jesus. He wants us to walk in a world-changing destiny.

LEARNING TO BE FAITHFUL
The Humility Test

It would not be practical to tell you all the tests I've been through, but I want to share a few to encourage you as you go through yours. One is a humility test that virtually anyone who is successful must go through because success tends to stir up pride in so many of us. I once asked R. T. Kendall if he had a word for me in 2001 at a conference in Columbus, Georgia—he was one of the spiritual fathers in my life—and he said, "Son, if you have more charisma and experience than you have character, I would see that as a warning sign." In other words, if your success is outpacing your testing and reliability, or if you go wider than you go deep, there will be tests to bring you back to humility. Humility is actually one of the kindest things God does for us because He gives grace to the humble but opposes the proud (Proverbs 3:34; James 4:6; 1 Peter 5:5). This is His way of ensuring that we receive His grace. Without Him, we can do nothing, but with Him, we can do all things. Our destiny comes from Him.

The Vulnerability Test

I've also experienced the test of vulnerability. If you heard only about my successes, mountaintop experiences, healings, and victories, you might assume I could not relate to your struggles and setbacks. I still sit in Chair 2 sometimes and have to get back into Chair 1. I have openly shared stories of some of my trials. I have experienced failures and struggled with things I thought I should have been able to overcome.

People need to see the reality of our lives with God. Certainly be vulnerable with Him, but also be vulnerable with the people around you. Let them see how He has worked in your life.

The Faithfulness Test

Another test is the faithfulness test. If you're faithful with a little, God gives you more. The good news with this test is that if you fail, you don't get kicked out of school. The bad news is that you can repeat the same grade again and again. I know some people who have been in first grade for 40 years, and they are either frustrated with God or resigned to what they think is a lesser destiny. One of my faithfulness tests was being a spiritual son to Jack Taylor. It took about five years of being a son of blessing before I became a son of inheritance. This was significant because one of my callings was to be a father of fathers who are going to bless nations. There would be 100 nations; I had prophecies about that. In fact, I had much more prophecy than I had destiny. If even 10 percent of the prophecies I received came true, the world would never be the same. It's one thing to have a word over your life and another for that word to become flesh.

When Randy Clark prophesied over me that I was going to be a bulldozer going into the darkest areas of the world where the gospel had never been before, it was connected to my destiny. Heaven declared it, and what God wanted to do was manifested through power and fire. What I didn't realize at the time was that it came in seed form and required faith. Many people experience quite a bit of discomfort in the faithfulness period. That happened to me; I got a compression fracture in my neck. At one point I was sitting in a body cast. I looked like the opposite of my destiny. How could this be? *The enemy will try to do everything he can to stop a seed from growing and being birthed because he doesn't want the prophetic word to become destiny.* He comes to kill, steal, and destroy, and he is always after our destiny. He never fulfilled his destiny, and he wants to keep others from fulfilling theirs. He's a dream-killer. The way to overcome is to be faithful in a little, and then you will be entrusted with more.

The Relationship Test

Another test is the relationship test. What does a covenant relationship look like? So some of my most painful lessons have been in learning to do relationships well. Because communication is such an integral part of relationships, I've been tested for many years in that area over and over again. I had to learn how to be a son before I could be a father, and that was a very long test. If I had only been a son of blessing, I would have only fathered sons of blessings, but today I'm fathering sons of inheritance. Many of them are carrying and transforming nations. My ceiling has become their floor. And I believe that before I'm gone, there will be at least 12 people with greater anointing, giftings, and capacity, who will have gone deeper and wider than I ever have. That is part of the destiny—and the legacy—I'm living for. My destiny is not about me. It's about "we."

There have been many other tests: learning how to be part of a royal priesthood; learning how to balance being a lamb, a lion, and an eagle, and knowing the rhythm of heaven so you can know which face is needed at which times; learning how to love well, which of course gets tested with the people closest to you; learning how to forgive and not carry an offense; all of these are part of the training-for-reigning program. If I'm going to be an ambassador of love and carry it into some of the darkest places in the world, it only makes sense that I would be tested in these areas and more. There are tests of power, perseverance, prophecy, and many others—the list could go on and on. You will face many of these tests for your destiny too. Though you often move up a grade, you never actually graduate. There will always be more tests. I'm again in the middle of one of these tests right now. They continue for a good reason – so I can grow in my capacity to steward greater inheritance. Who you become in the secret places of testing will eventually be revealed in the open.

Some of you may be in the royal priesthood test right now. As a priest on the inside in order to be a king on the outside, you have to learn when to be a priest and when to be royal. You may be trying to be a lion or an eagle on the outside while God is testing for you to be a lamb on the inside, or vice versa. It's important to realize what is going on in these times of testing so that you can respond well. The beautiful thing is that when you pass a test, you have a testimony to carry with you.

Your anointing will always be tested, because anointing rests on the assignment, and assignment is connected to destiny. That is why there needs to be alignment for the assignment. When I go out of alignment and the flow is interrupted, I have to ask who I am not in alignment with—in the natural and the spiritual. I have spiritual fathers in my life, but I also have spiritual sons and daughters. It's very important to learn how to be a family or community together because it affects destiny.

BUILDING BRIDGES; DIGGING VALLEYS

A couple of years before I turned 50, our ministry passed a one million mark. For 18 years, it had cost me everything to be away from my wife and children to go into the darkest places in the world. It's great to see a breakthrough, but there's a price that comes with it. We saw a million names added to the Lamb's book of life, and 300,000 people healed. When all of these things happen before you turn 50, and you stand on top of the mountain and recall all the words that had been spoken over your life, it's amazing. Then you think, *"Where do I go from here?"* The tendency is to think you've arrived, that you've fulfilled your destiny. While man builds bridges, God digs valleys.

I enjoyed that mountaintop experience for a while because it was as much as I knew at that point in my life, until I realized that my destiny was not getting to the top of that mountain; it was the daily journey I had experienced with God. I had learned to get the muscles and body and heart functioning together, to connect with people and be in the presence of God. I knew how to be in the secret place, to establish identity, to cultivate intimacy, to recognize what is available in our inheritance, and how we have favor with God and men because I had been tested in these areas. All of these tests have taught me valuable lessons about honoring people who dishonor you, how to be a son to Pharaohs, what it takes to go into the Muslim world, and how to add value for other people to experience.

Being A Dream Releaser

I was a speaker at a conference at Bethel Church in Redding, California, several years ago, and I sensed the Holy Spirit speaking to me between sessions. "Leif, I want you to go back to the bookstore, but this time without buying anything."

My wonderful friends at Bethel were always so generous to say, "Leif, whatever you want." They would be extravagant with resources and tools to help me in my ministry. However, this time the Holy Spirit was clear. "I want you to see how you can add value to what you honor."

God wanted me to understand that we aren't to come to the family table and eat only what someone else has prepared. We are to bring something to the table for others. How can I add value to the people in other ministries? How can I add value to the spiritual fathers in my life? My staff? My sons and daughters? Those questions became another test toward my destiny. It is not just about what I am called to do but about others too. How can I help them fulfill their destiny? *Beyond fulfilling my dream, how can I be a dream releaser for others?* More than soaring as an eagle myself, how can I raise up a culture of eagle Christians who will take the seven spheres or mountains of society? How can I help others experience the supernatural in addition to experiencing it myself? I love seeing people get out of their eagle's nest for the first time when they experience the supernatural and begin to stretch their wings and soar. They sharpen their talons and their vision and go after serpents around the world. It is a joy as a father to hear the stories of both my natural and spiritual children, realizing their destiny and joy are connected to my destiny and joy. God often expands our vision in the tests we go through and the principles He teaches us.

I want to live full and die empty, to do everything God has called me to do.

Inheritance is not just for receiving; it's for passing down to the next generation. Our connections are not just for now; they apply across generations. I had grandparents and other forebears who are in heaven and were not able to fulfill everything they envisioned, but I am connected to them. They are at the command center in heaven and are looking down at us. They are that large cloud of witnesses mentioned in Hebrews 12:1 who paid a price and passed on the torch. The same is true if I look ahead. I have a short time here on earth to fulfill everything I envision, and that is my heart's desire. I want to be known as a son but also to be a father of nations. I believe we will see 100 nations in our generation transformed by power, wisdom, and love. That's why we have been raising up Chair 1 believers for over a decade and teaching people how to have Chair 1 marriages and businesses. I want people to know what a Chair 1 education looks like, to see heaven's creativity flow out of people who have captured their identity and gone into the secret place of intimacy. I want sons and daughters to grow into maturity and move into a place of inheritance, where they learn how to honor well and love well. We need to think beyond destiny and into legacy.

STEWARDING EDEN

The wording of Genesis 2:8 suggests that when God planted Eden on earth, He was establishing a portion of heaven's realm in earth's environment. Humanity's mission was to take that environment and expand its borders. Whenever we get a glimpse of heaven—in worship, in an encounter with God, in a testimony or revelation, in a miracle or move of His Spirit—it's a portal into another realm. If we recognize it and steward it, we can increase it. We can take anything of God's kingdom culture and use it to shape the world around us. We can increase Eden, the environment of heaven, on earth.

That's our role as habitations of the Dove and carriers of the family's glory. *We have been given the privilege and responsibility to steward God's presence—to guard and value what we have experienced with Him and multiply it.* Yes, there will be tests, but they are actually opportunities for upgrade and will turn into testimonies. They prepare us to be culture changers—and to spread the peace of Eden into a restless world.

CHAPTER THIRTEEN DEVOTIONAL
Destiny

God has a dream and Holy Spirit has a vision - for every person to experience a God who looks like Jesus and loves like Jesus. That's a picture of Kingdom family. There are many things involved in being part of God's family – faithfulness, vulnerability, humility, relationship. It is likely that all of us will be tested in those areas at some point because our destiny is not getting to the top of that mountain; it's the daily journey we experience with God. He wants us to learn how to steward Eden well with Him; to be a dream-releaser like Him. To do that we need to get past pride, shame, and the frustration of unfaithfulness that are part of life. The good news is that God is always there to help and equip us for every challenge. He is a good, good Father who has good things for His children.

FOCUS AREAS

» The Humility Test – success tends to stir up pride.

» The Vulnerability Test – people need to see the reality of our lives with God.

» The Faithfulness Test – discomfort is common in the faithfulness period.

» The Relationship Test – destiny is not about "me," it's about "we" – you and God and the family of God.

REFLECTIONS

Humility is something we all struggle with. Don't be discouraged if you haven't quite gotten it down yet. Look to Jesus as your example, and ask Holy Spirit to speak to your heart regarding your own humility.

Vulnerability is another area that is challenging for most people. Yet, when we are willing to share our stories, God gets the glory. If you haven't stepped out in that area, give it a try. God will meet you and bless your efforts.

Relationships can pose some of the biggest challenges for us in the church because churches are typically hospitals for sinners not museums for saints.[1] We bring our wounds and expect to be loved, and when it doesn't always work that way, people get hurt. One way to deal with relationships is to continually allow Holy Spirit to conform your mind to the mind of Christ. When we think like the Father thinks, and put on the Son-glasses and see as He sees, relationship issues are more easily dealt with.

---

1 Augustine of Hippo, John Chrysostom, and Abigail Van Buren, among others, are credited with having made this statement.

CHAPTER FOURTEEN
Culture Changers

King Nebuchadnezzar of Babylon had a dream about a great tree that was cut down to a stump and then allowed to grow again. Daniel had proven to be a faithful adviser because he had not only interpreted an earlier dream for the king, but he actually told the king what the dream was in the first place. As a result, Nebuchadnezzar trusted him and so he called upon Daniel to interpret this dream too. The king recognized the Spirit of God in this captive from Israel.

Daniel received an interpretation from God, but it was not good news for the king. The dream symbolized Nebuchadnezzar himself. He would be cut down and brought low for a time, only to have his kingdom restored to him once he recognized God. Daniel was deeply troubled by the interpretation. Not only did he not want to tell this news to Nebuchadnezzar; he didn't even want it to happen. "My lord, if only the dream applied to your enemies and its meaning to your adversaries!" he said (Daniel 4:19). He was grieved about the judgment that was coming. His heart was burdened for a pagan king.

BE A BLESSING

This story is one example of how sons and daughters walk out their destiny. Because we know that the mission of our Father is a family mission, we do not stand against the world in judgment. We are for the world. Our hearts are invested in those we love, honor, and serve. We are always asking the question, "How can I be a blessing?" because we know it's the heart of our Father to bless—and because, in our alignment with Him, He has put the desire to bless into our hearts as well.

This is not the perspective of Chair 2 believers. Chair 2 Christians are often asking, "How can I get a blessing out of this situation? What can this church or this person do for me?" If you have a Chair 1 church that is filled with Chair 1 members, they don't come to see what they can get but to see what they can give. They are not asking, "How can I be blessed?" but rather, "How can I be a blessing?" They don't just come to get healed or to get a prophetic word; they want to know how to bring healing or speak God's heart into the lives of others.

This is the kind of people God is raising up in this day—not just in churches but in families, schools, businesses, governments, and more. If you really want to know how to bring honor and glory to God in this world become an agent of the Father's blessing.

KINGDOM CULTURE

In order to change a culture, we need to have a different culture within us.

Carry the Presence

Remember, we are carriers of the Dove's habitation and we live from heaven to earth. The rest of the world is living from earth toward heaven, hoping to get some of heaven's blessings and resources into their lives. We are already in the Father's house; He has already said, "All that I have is yours." We are agents who bring those resources and solutions into every area of our world. We carry the atmosphere of heaven—the love and honor we have experienced in the Father's living room—for others around us to experience.

We can't impart what we don't have. Daniel and his friends understood who they were and who they belonged to. The culture within them shaped the culture around them. Culture changers know who they are, whose they are, what they have, and what they are called to do—to be a chosen nation and a royal priesthood (1 Peter 2:9). They also know what is happening in this world and look for opportunities to bless and carry *shalom* into restless, anxious, and even dark places. As priests, we re-present God before the people and the people before God. As sons and daughters of the King, we carry keys of the kingdom to bind and loose and prophesy the King's decrees. Those are all intercessory roles, and they flow from the intimacy we have with the Father. From that intimacy, we take on the responsibility of ruling and reigning with Him. Our place of habitation becomes a kingdom culture, and our culture brings the blessings of love, honor, and covenant. The increase of the kingdom and the government of *shalom* are going to be on the shoulders of the Son (Isaiah 9:7)—and the sons and daughters.

This kingdom culture is first and foremost a family culture—not an institutional culture, not an organizational agenda, and not a religious movement. If the fellowship of Father, Son, and Spirit in heaven is the prototype for earth, as we saw in Eden, then heaven's environment on earth is going to look like that fellowship. We will still honor people we disagree with, love those who are not yet receptive to our love, and bless those who might expect us to curse them. That's what the prayer "On earth as it is in heaven" (Matthew 6:10) is all about. We do this together with the Father, Son, and Spirit. It's a journey together as a family.

Live as Sons and Daughters of Glory

You can't change the environment unless you have already been changed by the Father's family environment.

When you represent heaven on earth with that spirit of fellowship, your stock suddenly goes up. I have seen this happen again and again in my work in the Muslim world. I am expected to be an adversary, but when I come in with a servant's towel as a lamb rather than a lion, carrying the ideas and solutions and atmosphere of heaven, I suddenly become a friend. I'm carrying a spirit of family. That gives me opportunities later to be a lion or an eagle, demonstrating boldness or wisdom from God, but you can't change the environment unless you first get into it.

We carry the kingdom culture into places where it is not yet established. To do that, we must come from an environment of peace in order to manifest peace. This often requires we go into a harsh environment as a lamb who has no other agenda than to bless with the blessings of heaven. Sons and daughters of glory have learned when to be a lamb, a lion, or an eagle—when to present themselves as servants, leaders, or wise counselors. We see this pattern in Scripture in people like Joseph, Daniel, and Nehemiah, who all had enormous influence within a pagan, orphan environment. They all carried the gift of sonship—not to mature, spiritual fathers but to people like Pharaoh, Nebuchadnezzar, and Artaxerxes. They were not antagonists toward their pagan leaders; they desired rather to bless them. They carried heaven's atmosphere into the dark places of earth. *They had the spirit of sons among orphans.*

That is why it is so important to capture your identity—to know who you are and live from that position. Then you can be entrusted with heaven's resources. God sets you up as a city on a hill, displaying the power and wisdom of love.

Be Pastors in the Marketplace

*God is raising up a generation of people who understand that ministry
is not something that happens just within the walls of a church.*

I've always had a weakness for cars. They are like one of my love
languages. When we lived in Alabama years ago, I would take my
car to a place every week to get it cleaned, and the guys there did
a beautiful job. The young man who owned the shop knew I was a
pastor and ministry leader. He would tell me often, "God has called
me to be a pastor. I'm eventually going to sell the business and go to
Bible college and seminary. I have a lot of prophetic words over my
life. Will you pray for me? I want to be faithful." For months, he told
me this, and I began to get to know him.

One day the Holy Spirit spoke to me and taught me something
I had to share with this young man. So the next time I saw him, I said,
"You *are* a pastor. Let me pray for you now, and I'll ordain you." He
had tears in his eyes. He had never thought of his employees as his
church members. Every car his company washed was touched with
the presence of God inside and out. He didn't realize he had more
lost people coming through his business every day than any church
does. He was meeting and influencing people with the kingdom as a
business owner. He was a pastor in the marketplace.

Many people have dreams of doing something unusual and
influential in the marketplace but don't realize that it qualifies as
ministry. If you have those kinds of dreams, they may be pointing to

your destiny, so too are the things you weep over when you watch the news or hear someone's story. If you could do anything without any fear of failure, what would you do? A special sensitivity to injustice, immorality, poverty, conflict, certain needs or problems, or anything else may tell you a lot about what you are called to do.

THE LAMB, THE LION AND THE EAGLE

I know people who carry the habitation of the Dove into small businesses, into the highest courts of government and power, and everywhere in between. One of the paradigms for bringing heaven's blessings and resources into earth is the picture of the Seven Mountains or Seven Spheres of society. I've seen two ways to approach that paradigm. One of them, which is sometimes called dominion theology, is simply about going into the mountains as believers, rising to high positions, and then leading from that place. However, if believers are carrying an orphan heart into their spheres of influence, we have a problem. Very often they take on the atmosphere of their surroundings rather than changing the atmosphere in that sphere. They know how to slay giants with a slingshot but not how to worship with a harp. We end up with leaders who may know what it takes to get to heaven but not how to bring heaven to earth. They have a desire to be culture changers but are trying to do it with the gospel of salvation and not the gospel of the kingdom—a much fuller, more comprehensive mission. All we have then is a group of people who know how to influence mountains and create a tipping point, but they are still carrying an orphan culture. That won't change the world.

When we come from a place of identity and intimacy first, we know we are representing our Father and His heart. We know what He thinks and feels and sees. From there, we know what is available to us—His love and honor, His wisdom, His peace, His provision. There is a top Muslim leader in Asia who calls me "father" because I have gone in with a family culture and the heart of a son, just as Joseph, Daniel, and Nehemiah were sons to Pharaoh, Nebuchadnezzar, and Artaxerxes but influenced them with heaven's wisdom.

A spirit of sonship and servanthood raises your stock, giving you a platform to represent God's heart while raising the stock of the rest of us.

KINGDOM ALIGNMENT FOR KINGDOM ASSIGNMENT

In Chair 1, we are not learning how to take mountains and get dominion. That may be a byproduct, but we really should be known as people whose only agenda is to bless with the blessings of heaven. When we go in as sons and daughters, we are entrusted with inheritance. We learn *the rhythm of love, power, and wisdom—the lamb, the lion, and the eagle.* The kingdom alignment that comes with that sets us up for the kingdom assignment we have been given.

What does heaven on earth look like in the seven spheres of society? If you're a schoolteacher, it means you can wake up in the morning thanking God for Mondays because you're going into a classroom setting where you can represent the Father. You carry heaven's environment into that place. Instead of seeing an ADHD problem in a student, you may see a destiny of creativity. Instead of seeing students who are bored, you see students who are primed to discover the thing that captures their heart. Instead of focusing on a child's restless or rebellious tendencies, you see an opportunity to bring *shalom*. You don't treat them based on their history but on their destiny.

If you're a nurse, you wake up realizing you have a unique opportunity to minister to people at difficult times in their lives. If you're an accountant, you can see the opportunity to demonstrate heaven's integrity as you handle earth's resources. One of my spiritual sons in our family realized he was a Chair 1 police officer. He goes into the secret place as a son and gets insights from the Father, then helps make connections between where drugs are coming from and going, how the enemy is strategizing in certain cities, and prevents many bad things from happening. People are amazed. We have story after story of this kind of thing happening with businessmen, neuroscientists, teachers, government workers, and more. They are lambs, lions, and eagles in every area of society.

CHAPTER FOURTEEN
DEVOTIONAL
Culture Changers

Sons and daughters in the Kingdom family become agents of the Father's blessings from Chair 1, which always asks, "How can I be a blessing?" When we carry the Kingdom culture of heaven within us, it impacts the culture around us. With the fellowship of the Trinity as our prototype we can help bring heaven to earth in every circumstance. It's all about living as a son or daughter of glory, always with a servant's towel over your arm. From this place of influence with God you will change the atmosphere in your spheres of influence. A spirit of sonship and servanthood raises your stock and gives you a platform to represent God's heart while raising the stock of everyone in the "family."

FOCUS AREAS

» Pastors in the Marketplace – God is raising up a generation who understands that ministry is not something that happens just within the walls of the church.

» Live as Sons and Daughters of Glory – speak to the orphan heart rather than carrying it; be the influencer, not the influenced.

» The Lamb, the Lion and the Eagle – learn the rhythm of love, power and wisdom.

REFLECTION QUESTIONS

1. Which question do you find yourself asking most often, "How can I be a blessing" or "How can I get a blessing"?

2. How hard is it for you to get into Chair 1 when it comes to being a culture changer? What are your greatest challenges in this area?

3. How hard is it for you to be a lamb, or a lion, or an eagle – to get into the rhythm of God's love, power and wisdom? Why?

CHAPTER FIFTEEN

Bringing Heaven to Earth

COVERT REVIVAL

You will not receive an anointing for an assignment you do not have, but the assignments you do have will be anointed with the presence of the Dove.

Most of the revival happening around the world is covert, not in big arenas with crowds of worshipers but in the corners and crevices of the marketplace. Your alignment for your assignment makes you a resting place for Him in whatever sphere He has placed you in, and things happen to bring heaven's environment to earth.

God will give you clarity on these things through the dreams you have with Him. Learning to dream with God is a key part of your alignment, and it comes in two ways. First, God wants to bring things of heaven into earth, and as a son or daughter, you will begin to see specifically what they are. As you delight in Him in the place of intimacy, you will find your desire for Him manifesting in the desires of your own heart—your heart merges with His to desire the things that are unique to your calling and personality. What are the things you would like to do? As a mature son or daughter, He can entrust you with those things. He will take you shopping. He loves having a family He can dream with.

When you delight in God and dream with Him and then He fulfills your desires, others are able to see who your Father is. They want to know a Papa like that. Orphan hearts—whether they are in Islam, Hinduism, secularism, or the church—long for that kind of connection and synchronization with the Father. They want intimacy and are looking for it in all the wrong places. A Chair 1 worldview changes how we see them, feel about them, and think about them. As a result, it changes how people see the Father.

THE REFORMATION

In chapter 8 I mentioned three reformations. The first was 500 years ago. After many forerunners prepared the ground for what was to come, Martin Luther sparked a reformation in how people saw God and understood salvation. For centuries, many people thought the only way to get salvation was through works, and if they wanted to have a relationship with God, they would need a priest as an intermediary. Luther emphasized salvation by grace through faith alone and fought for universal access to God's Word. Many reformers like Wycliffe or Tyndale paid a high price for you and me to have access to the Bible and relate directly to God. The Reformation expanded the Renaissance that was taking place. We can actually connect the later development of a middle class and widespread literacy around the world to what was happening in this time. It changed the world forever.

One of the weaknesses of the Luther reformation was that in protesting doctrines, they became very doctrinal themselves. They often positioned themselves doctrinally opposite of the Catholic Church, and sought unity in Protestant doctrinal matters. "We don't believe that; we believe this instead." The reasoning and discovery that came out of that movement accomplished wonderful things— doctrinal clarity, educational institutions, publishing industries, and more—and we can be thankful to God for that. Hunger for the Word of God led many people to study it and anchor themselves in its truth. But some of the doctrinal divisions—even to the point of people finding their identity in doctrinal positions—created an imbalance in that reformation. We have found in the last 500 years that when we say, "Doctrine is what unifies us," we end up with thousands upon thousands of denominations, many of which will not even associate with one another. When we say, "We can have fellowship only if we believe the same thing on this or that issue," we end up getting divorced. Then we split off and start another orphanage that we call a church.

One of the core values of the Reformation was education—in itself, a wonderful emphasis—but the education system that came out of it to train teachers and pastors often categorized them in ways that furthered division. The family of God became doctrinally exclusive, not relationally inclusive. Protestants were right to protest, but one of the problems in a protest that splits you from your heritage is that you end up fatherless. God wanted to restore more than right beliefs. He wanted to preserve and restore the family of His sons and daughters.

I praise God for that first reformation. One thing that concerns me about Spirit-led movements today is that many people who have come into them don't have a plumb line any longer. They don't know what God says about things. That's a problem because everything from Genesis to Revelation comes alive when you have the right glasses on. For this generation to move in the inheritance and destiny God has for us, we need to be able to see Scripture clearly. If you overemphasize the Word without the life of the Spirit, you begin to dry up. When you bring them together, you grow up. I am grateful for the Baptist college and seminary I went to because I got rooted in the first reformation and in the Word of God. The first reformation was very important; we need doctrine, and we need to be rooted in grace. But doctrine is not what defines us.

THE SECOND GREAT AWAKENING

The next reformation was the revival that began in the early 1900s. God began speaking to people around the world—Wales, South Africa, the United States, and others—to prepare hearts. William Seymour became a catalyst for the Azusa Street revival, which in turn was a catalyst for a vast spiritual movement that would grow into what we know as Pentecostalism and the Charismatic renewal. The emphases in this reformation were the Holy Spirit and His gifts, and we see much of the fruit today as people move in gifts that had long been ignored in the church. Even the ideas of intimacy with the Father and receiving an inheritance were not widely entertained in the centuries leading up to the 1900s, though there were certainly exceptions. But while we see numerous visitations and encounters with God before then, we don't see many experiences of habitation.

The Holy Spirit has always been around, but it took a reformation for people to access Him continually.

There had been many revivals that touched communities, but revival doesn't transform culture. Reformation does. The Holy Spirit reformation of the 20th century was a culture reformation, and the world has never gone back. Remember what we said earlier about what we value? *If we value, we can steward; and if we steward, we can multiply; and if we multiply, we get authority.* It is very important to value what earlier reformations have given us. I see the first reformation as being about Jesus, and the second as being about the Holy Spirit. I am grateful to God for both. Many people paid a price—rejection, opposition, and sometimes even their own lives—in both of those periods of change. There was weakness in the second reformation just as there was in the first. Just as one of the core values in the first reformation was doctrine, one of the core values of the second is anointing. Who do people want in the pulpit? One who demonstrates power; one with the gifts? The more anointing someone can demonstrate, the more value others put in that person. What if the anointed and gifted ones don't yet see themselves as sons and daughters? What if they haven't yet prioritized intimacy with the Father? What if they are going after inheritance before they are mature? The Holy Spirit has been poured out in abundance for generations, but we have not yet changed the world. The reason is that many of those who have received the outpouring still have orphan hearts. We adopted fathers who never learned how to be sons.

The family of Father, Son, Spirit, and sons and daughters who know who and whose they are is meant to bless all the nations of the earth. Chair 2 believers have long seen their assignment to make disciples in terms of teaching individuals so that they can have an encounter with God. Chair 1 focuses on discipling nations by leading individuals into an encounter with God and then teaching them. That is a very different way.

A NEW REFORMATION

The first reformation restored grace, and the second power.
This new reformation will restore love.

A new reformation is coming. The church is in a time of transition. *We are no longer who we used to be, but we have not yet become who we are supposed to become.* That is true for us as a body and as individuals, and many are feeling the tension. No one is surprised that Chair 3 is being shaken, but Chair 2 is being shaken also. The kingdom in Chair 1 is unshakeable, however, and Jesus is unchanging. Our mission is like playing a game where we already know the final score. We can be perfectly content because we see the end. I can go into the darkest places of the world and be at peace because I know what is happening. It's like inside trading, but in the kingdom, it's legal. We have a new way of fishing—not making an intellectual argument but helping people have an encounter with Jesus and experience His love. That's the focus of our worldwide mission in the third reformation.

The core value in this next reformation is not the gifts of the individual. In the previous reformation, people came to the family table to eat whatever the anointed ones brought to it. Those with the strongest gifts were the focus. *Now leaders are adding value to others by investing in their gifts.* They are realizing that anyone can do these things. They are creating a ceiling for others to use as their floor. We are starting to see this new "baby" being born all around the world. The Old Testament ends with a promise of the spirit of Elijah, which will restore the hearts of fathers toward their children and children toward their fathers.

Restored love will stop the curse in the land. *Love will take self out of the worldwide orphanage and put family in its place.* Jesus prayed that the perfect love the Father has for the Son would be in each one of us (John 17:26). Then we will love ourselves the way He loves us, which will enable us to love our neighbors as we love ourselves. When that is coupled with the power of the second reformation, we will see a love that changes everything. That has been the missing piece.

TAKING FAMILY CULTURE INTO AN ORPHAN WORLD

Bringing the best of each reformation into your assignment
and adding the love of the Father to the power and the Word
are what it takes to be a culture changer.

Changing culture is not about me and my anointing or you and yours. When the stock of one of us goes up, all of our stock goes up. When one of us has a breakthrough, we all have a breakthrough. When one has a great prophetic word or a miraculous provision, we think, "Wow, that's my brother, that's my sister," not, "Why did that person get it and I didn't?" We are no longer orphans who think that way. We are a family coming to the family table, and we are taking the family culture into an orphan world. We do it as those who are on a mission to restore love because that is the Father's ultimate purpose. From a place of identity and intimacy, we demonstrate the love, power, and wisdom of God through signs, wonders, and miracles. *The reformation within us and among us will change the culture around us.*

Chair 1 is always a place of rest. It's home. It's a place where sons and daughters are living, not just visiting. It is actually living in the environment of heaven while on earth, from a position of being seated with Christ in heavenly places. In that place, we have the proper identity and enjoy intimacy with the Father. The Dove comes and rests on us. It's a place of face-to-face encounter, where we become prophetic people because we are hearing His voice. Even more than that, we know His heart, feel His heartbeat, and have the wisdom to know what to do with a prophetic word. God is raising up a generation of people who live in this place of identity and intimacy and who will flow in their inheritance in wisdom, power, and love.

We don't have to strive to get to this place. We already have an A+ on our report card before we even take the test. We've made the 3-point shot before we let go of the ball because we're no longer living under pressure but from the Father's pleasure. Whether we score or not is not the issue; what matters is that we're out there playing ball and having fun. Even when things get difficult, we can consider it all joy because trials and obstacles lead to upgrades in our training-for-reigning program. We are free to dream with God and expect those dreams to become destiny. To do that, we need to understand the inheritance available to us in this season of history. The great cloud of witnesses paid a price for this day. We are standing on their shoulders, and we are setting something up for the next generation.

DREAM RELEASERS

The destinies of those who have gone before are connected to our destiny today, and our destiny today is connected to the destinies of those who are coming.

The quickest way to find our own destiny is to be dream-releasers for others. That's the promise of the resting place. There is no better promise than the destiny of a son or daughter of God in the resting place. We receive love and release it. We experience joy and share it. We enter into peace and give it away. We enjoy the presence of God and carry it for others to enjoy. We establish Chair 1 marriages and businesses and show the world another way to live that is neither rebellious nor religious but at home in the Father's house. From that place, we can thank God for Monday mornings because we know we are taking the Dove, the presence, and the favor of God into the workplace. We can face challenges—a difficult boss, a persistent problem, an unfair situation—as opportunities to change the environment. We can show people what it's like to keep our love on, to ooze the Spirit when we get squeezed, to pass tests and have a testimony, and to be thankful for the 40 hours a week we get to influence the marketplace. A believer who is faithful in those relationships will be faithful with his destiny.

So what is God up to? Where is He inviting you to join Him? How do you fit into His bigger picture? Where and how does He want you to reign? These are questions to sort out in the secret place in your intimate conversations with Him. Ask Him to help you understand the time you are living in. Many people throughout history have not understood the seasons and missed out on what God was doing. They didn't know how to join Him in His work. When you understand the times, you see His invitation for destiny. You step into it. And yes, you can be trusted to carry it.

CHAPTER FIFTEEN
DEVOTIONAL
Bringing Heaven to Earth

There are covert revivals and overt revivals. God may call you to one or the other depending on where He wants you at a particular time. No matter where He calls you, remember two things: you will not receive an anointing for an assignment you do not have, and the assignments you are given will be anointed with the presence of the Dove. Moving between assignments is easier as you learn to dream with God. The Bible is full of dreamers. Their destinies are connected to your destiny today, and your destiny is connected to those who will come after you. When we take the best of the past and bring it into our current assignments, add the love of the Father and the power of the Word, we will find ourselves among the ranks of God's change agents. Kingdom change agents are reformers who bring the love that stops the curse and ushers in the culture of heaven.

FOCUS AREAS

Three Reformations

» The Luther Reformation – restored grace. Salvation by grace through faith alone, universal access to God's word. Protected doctrine while becoming very doctrinal, which created divisions causing the family of God to become doctrinally exclusive, not relationally inclusive.

» Second Great Awakening – restored power. About the Holy Spirit and His gifts. Holy Spirit has always been with us, but it took a reformation for people to access Him continually.

» The New Reformation – restoring love. Love will take self out of the worldwide orphanage and put family in its place.

REFLECTION QUESTIONS

1. Why do you think it is important for the church to protect doctrine?

2. What are some of the dreams you want to dream with God?

3. How do you see your destiny connected to those who are coming behind you?

CHAPTER SIXTEEN
Living in a Kingdom Culture

SHIPWRECKED

I was coming home from a trip to Tanzania in 2005, and I had been experiencing a lot of breakthroughs, miracles, and healings. Yet I also had a lot of dysfunction. I was in pain—physically and emotionally. There was a black hole in my soul that I hadn't dealt with. I had been on opiates for nine years because of numerous surgeries and back pain, and my use had turned to abuse for the last two of those years, mainly to survive. Pain always seeks pleasure. As I mentioned in chapter 9, I ended up in a treatment center, and the next five months were the darkest and hardest season of my life. I was stuck in Chair 2 and did not know how to get out.

As I was getting off of opiates, I was crippled by pain and fear, as if dark clouds were always over my head. I was depressed. For part of that season, I was afraid I was going to die. Then I was afraid I wasn't going to die. Things even got worse. It was my cave of Adullam experience—as with David, a key part of my upgrade. I just didn't know that then. I didn't realize God was setting me up for what was to come.

I knew I was a son of Papa God. I'd had my baptism of love, had experienced anointing and giftings, and had a worldwide ministry speaking at some of the best conferences in the world. But I still had the black hole in my soul, a place that had not yet been touched by perfect love. I still didn't know how to live a life without medication. I couldn't travel or sleep without medication, and it had been that way for 11 years.

In May 2006, I was speaking at a healing school with Bill Johnson and Randy Clark at a Lutheran church in Minnesota. This was one of my first times of ministering after my season of shipwreck, when all my "ships"—apostleship, leadership, stewardship, relationships, etc.—got wrecked. Only sonship remained. I was giving five messages at that conference, and while I was there the organizers asked if I could meet with a small group from the Philippines. "They are tired, burned out, and beaten up," I was told. "They have heard some of your story, especially how God is using you in the Muslim world, and they wanted to meet you and have you pray for them. They are expecting God to touch them."

I ended up in a side room with this group between sessions. We had lunch together, I showed them some videos, and we started to talk. They saw on the videos how 22,000 people in the darkest places of the world had been touched by heaven. They saw an example of

Chair 1. The problem was that I only knew how to visit. I couldn't stay in Chair 1 because of the black hole in my soul.

I went around the room and prayed for everyone in this group. I touched them and blessed them, and everyone felt something. Three in particular looked like they had been hit with a sledgehammer from heaven. When they came up from the floor later, they showed me their hands. Two of them, Paul and Ahlmira Yadao, had oil flowing out of their hands. Those are the kinds of signs that make you wonder! I knew God was doing something unusual. I just didn't know what it was.

Later during the conference, Paul and Ahlmira came up to me in a hallway and asked if I would be their spiritual father. They had come looking for that from one of us—they didn't know which leader it would be, but they wanted someone to father them—and realized that my messages about the orphan spirit and orphanage churches resonated with them. They used my language to describe what was going on: "We have experienced Chair 1 revival in the past, but we didn't know how to let it stay. We are primarily a Chair 2 church. We have been living for God, but we need a father in our lives who can give us a father's blessing."

To be honest, I was just focused on being a son in this season of my life. I had been a father to some people before, but I did not feel prepared for that kind of relationship at this time. I had not yet learned how to stay in Chair 1 either. So I said, "Well, I am coming to the Philippines at the end of next year. Perhaps then . . ."

"We cannot wait that long!" Ahlmira said. "Please."

So I gave them a father's blessing, and when I did, something exploded. I didn't realize it at the time, but it was what the first part of this book is all about: identity. When I kissed them and said, "You are my beloved son, my beloved daughter," something was unlocked. They described it later as an explosion that was somehow connected to their destiny. (Today their ministry is called Destiny Ministry International.) They had a baptism of love and experienced being sons and daughters of Papa God. I was just a spiritual father in the natural realm who believed in them.

I was in Nashville the next month with my natural son Leif Emmanuel when I got a phone call. "Hey, Daddy Leif! Happy Father's Day!" I had to ask who it was; I had forgotten because I go from conference to conference and meet a lot of people. They said, "This is your son and daughter from the Philippines! Can you come and visit us?" Just a week earlier I had been invited to speak at a huge conference that would be a fulfilled dream for anyone in ministry—a "who's who" team of leaders, and I would have been the seventh speaker among them. It was a first-class ticket, a nice honorarium, and a great opportunity. The Holy Spirit said, "I want you to say no. You do not have time for big conferences, but you do have time for family." So instead of speaking at the dream conference with some of the world's foremost Christian speakers, I left the U.S. in the back of a plane with no medication and lots of pain to meet two people I really didn't know. I had met them at a conference and prayed a father's blessing over them, and the Spirit called them family. They were a son and a daughter.

We spent the next few days together hanging out and trying to help them establish their understanding of who they were and whose they were. They asked if I could also meet with their spiritual sons and daughters. "They also need a baptism of love and a father's blessing," they said. So we met, and I still remember a wind blowing in the meeting and some unusual things that happened. Before long, the baptism of love came in. They felt the affirmation of the Father and His liquid love filling them, and it changed the atmosphere. About 400 of them were just lying there getting their identity established as sons and daughters of a loving God. They felt the love of their Father in the spiritual realm, and they saw Paul and Ahlmira in the natural realm not as people trying to lead a movement but as a father and mother who could lead from sonship and daughtership.

Over the next few days, we focused totally on identity. They were trying to figure out from the old Chair 2 paradigm how to get a Chair 1 identity, and I didn't yet have the language to explain this. I was still trying to just be a son myself. So we asked a lot of questions. What does family look like? What does interdependence look like in the church? We began looking at these things, and this is how I became a student of what God was doing in this journey rather than just experiencing it. I barely knew these people but was beginning to love them as family. We learned a lot of together.

SOWING SEEDS

The second year I visited them—and I've been every year for the last decade now—I was speaking to more than 600 people when everyone started to point at me. I didn't see what was happening; I was starting to wonder if my zipper was down or something. What they were seeing were three very large orange feathers floating over my head. Finally, Paul yelled from the front row, "Daddy Leif, look above your head!" I looked up and saw the feathers too and was so overwhelmed. Gold dust started appearing on people's hands too. I was amazed and actually kept those feathers as a sign and wonder. The Filipinos were a little wiser and searched the video after the event. "What was Daddy Leif saying when the feathers appeared?" they wanted to know! They wanted to capture the thought and see why God was on it the way He was. What they discovered was that the feathers appeared when I said, "You're moving from an organization and institution, and you're going to be a family." When I said the word "family," something clicked in them. We talk a lot about church as a family, but what does that really look like? How do sons and daughters really live in community? What does a family business look like? A family of husband, wife, and children? I had given them a seed, and they took it and began a process of exploring these things.

On my visit the next year, I sat with a group of people in the conference. I began to weep because I was seeing not the identity of individuals but of couples, of children, of generations coming together. I saw businesses that were families, and it looked like heaven on earth. These were the beginnings of a long journey together as this identity and community have grown. I invited Paul to go to Pakistan with me, and he saw more than 20,000 people receive Jesus. Lame people were walking and the blind were seeing. Paul saw the atmosphere changing—literally heaven invading earth. When several hundred persecuted church leaders came to him he felt inadequate to bring a shift to that dark environment. The whole experience was almost like a culture shock for him. He left with a strong conviction, not from fear but from love, that he needed something more from heaven to be able to bring heaven to earth.

Paul went into the presence of God every night. He spent hours and hours, often from midnight to 4 a.m., just being alone with God. He was developing intimacy. He started going into the secret place and getting secrets. He went deeper before he went wider. I don't know anyone in the world who goes deeper than he does into the heart of God. He has such a strong identity as a son, and Paul and Ahlmira have become an amazing spiritual father and mother because of how they have grown as a son and daughter. I began to see what God has done through these beginnings of the Kingdom Family Movement as they got their identity and developed their intimacy. The whole movement has gone, and continues to go, deep into the presence and glory of God.

On one trip to Africa, I looked at Paul and told him he would be getting a release from heaven and lay hands on the sick. There were about 10,000 people there. Paul is a little more introverted than I am; where I have a tendency to go in as a lion sometimes, he is much more of a lamb! He is so trusting. We ministered as father and son together, and I still remember one girl who had come with scars all over her body. She had been cutting herself. The scars just disappeared. We realized this is what the father-son paradigm looks like and what love looks like. When you look with love, the scars disappear because Jesus took them on Himself at the cross. There was something about our intimacy with the Father and our intimacy in ministering together that released love and power. Paul had learned worship. He had spent four hours a day over a 10-year period just being alone with God, and he became like the One he was with. There was so much presence and anointing on him, so much glory. He carried the weight of revelation and unfolded things in Scripture I had never seen before. I became a student not just of him but of the culture that was being created, and I desired it too.

Paul and Ahlmira live out this intimacy in their marriage and with their children. Their two children are older now, but I remember years ago just lying on the floor and letting them lie on top of me, all of us just soaking in the presence of God. The children took me into some of the deepest places I have ever been in heavenly realms—pure streams and deep wells. I could still feel it hours afterward. I will never forget what I have seen in their family—what intimacy with God looks like in the flesh, and how it is released into destiny.

CHAIR 1 IN YOUR WORLD

Many of the stories I've shared are examples of what a Chair 1 lifestyle can look like, and I hope you experience similar adventures. These can be very calling-specific. Most Chair 1 experiences are common to all of us, regardless of calling. We've mentioned Chair 1 marriages, business, and churches, but specifically what do these look like? How do our identity, intimacy, inheritance, and destiny apply in everyday life?

Marriage

I'm convinced of who I am as a son, and I feel my Father's love, see His face, hear His voice, experience His presence, and abide in His pleasure. I know He is already well pleased with me, not based on what I do but simply for who I am. I have already received His blessing. Like Eve, who spent time with the Father before she was brought to Adam, my wife has had the same experience with the Father that I have. We have the Father's blessing together. We both already have an A+ from Him on our report cards. I'm Daddy's little boy, and she's Daddy's little girl. We both know whose we are. I can love my wife unconditionally because that's the way the Father loves me. She doesn't have to meet all my emotional needs because I know the Father will take care of me and His storehouse is full.

If I make a mistake—we will still experience the fall, after all—I'm not going to blame my wife, nor am I going to justify myself. I don't have to because I walk in humility. I can say, "I'm so sorry. I didn't honor you the way I should have." When both people in a marriage get their love, value, purpose, and affirmation from their intimacy with the Father, they don't look to each other to provide all of those things all the time. As the Father, Son, and Spirit do, we can celebrate each other's differences while also living in unity. We don't focus on the other person's deficiencies. We major on each other's gifts and potential. As a CEO friend reminded me once, God is not only your Father; He's also your Father-in-law. I'm married to Daddy's little girl. The way I treat her affects His favor toward me. That makes a huge difference in how I see my wife.

That doesn't mean we don't revert to Chair 2 every once in a while. Of course we do. But we don't stay there. We remind ourselves, "This is not normal. It is not the way God intended." When I stop hearing His voice, one of the first things I check after my intimacy with Him is my relationship with Jennifer. When I see His face, I see other people—especially her—differently. The biggest thing to remember in a Chair 1 marriage is that marriage is not a contract. It's a covenant. That means our love is not dependent on what the other person does. It's unconditional. We have become one with each other and are growing deeper into that unity. When she hurts, I hurt. When she is blessed, I feel joy. We don't compete with each other; we complete each other. We don't just tolerate each other; we celebrate each other. Looking out for each other's interests is in our own best interests.

This carries over to children too. When you're raising Chair 1 children, you always look for the gold in them and nurture it. You guide them, not control them. Over time, you help them move from being children of blessing to children of inheritance. You give them father's and mother's blessings. You can be vulnerable enough to admit when you reacted in Chair 2 and apologize for it. That humility doesn't diminish your authority; it actually enhances it. God gives grace to the humble, and as a parent, I need a lot of grace. It isn't hard to repent and get back into Chair 1. That's part of imparting a family culture to your children and eventually through them.

Business

A Chair 1 business operates on a father-son or father-daughter model. I know several CEOs who say Father God has 51 percent of the shares. It's His business. So they ask the Father what He wants to do and how He wants to treat people. One of them took a huge problem to the Lord, and the Lord answered, "Excuse Me, what problem?" The CEO went through a long description of the problem before he realized how much it sounded like Chair 2. He repented, "I'm sorry, Lord. It's Your problem, not mine. This is Your business. What are You going to do about it? How do You want to handle it?" Then he was able to get peace and God's wisdom over the matter. It was incredibly liberating to realize it wasn't ultimately his responsibility. It was God's. The weight of it was on God's shoulders, not his.

God knows how to take care of a business. If it's a kingdom business, it's a family business. That's the culture. You may be a CEO, but you are called to father your business, not run it like a machine. You represent the core values of the Father, Son, and Spirit in the workplace. He's a generous Father, so what does that look like when Christmas bonuses roll around? He does everything with a spirit of excellence; so what does that look like in your processes and practices? He is an extremely creative God; so how do you let creativity flow in your workplace? Whatever is part of the culture of heaven— love, honor, blessing, rest, loyalty, faithfulness, excellence, creativity, generosity, grace, etc.—can flow into your business as you represent that culture there.

Church

Many of the principles that apply to families and businesses also apply to churches, with the addition that churches exist specifically to impart the kingdom culture and equip people to carry it into the other areas of their lives. We have seen how a Chair 1 church is not filled with people who are coming to get a blessing (though they probably will). It is filled with people who come to be a blessing. It is a family where people are welcomed not based on their agreement but on who they are; they are celebrated, not just tolerated. Religion has created rifts and separation because of disagreement, but the restoration of a Chair 1 church as Jesus intended is a place of unity in diversity. When people commit to a church from Chair 1, they come to the family table and offer their uniqueness to edify the body rather than receive affirmation. In the same way, when sons and daughters seated in Chair 1 are in positions of church leadership, their greatest desire is not to have the best church or the biggest platform but to see their sons and daughters, their family, step into their destiny and see their dreams realized. Chair 1 churches represent the kingdom family in such a way that it becomes an irresistible invitation for outsiders and an authentic voice to influence community.

These are a few areas where your identity and intimacy play out in everyday life, and I'm sure you can find ways to apply the principles to other areas too. The truth is that when we know who we are, whose we are, what we have, and what we are called to do, it changes everything—in every area of life—for ourselves and the people around us.

NEVER TOO LATE

I spent years as a pastor and ministry leader before understanding the difference between worldviews and how they affect identity, intimacy, inheritance, and destiny. I didn't have a paradigm of three chairs or heaven's blueprint. It would be easy to look back and regret all the years of missed opportunities to see as God sees, hear His voice, and walk through open doors He provides.

I encounter many people who have such regrets, and I tell them this: *you are not responsible for a revelation you didn't have.* Sure, I wish I could start my marriage in Chair 1, raise Chair 1 children, and lead a Chair 1 church. I didn't know any of that when I first got married or in the 1990s when I was a pastor. I knew the Word, but I did not always know the Spirit, at least not very well. I knew Jesus and was saved, sealed, and secure. The Spirit was in me, but not upon me. Then I got to know Papa, and things changed. I discovered my identity. He invited me into the house from the fields where I had been laboring. I have to believe that His timing was right for me. Nothing before was wasted, and everything afterward builds on the journey with Him.

Remember Paul Yadao? One of his children was very upset with him because she did not get to experience the benefits of his new relationship with the Father when she was young. I've seen this again and again from adult children who lament that their parents did not behave in a particular way with them. He said, "Could it be that I just didn't know how to love this way? I am sorry for that. But can you give me a chance now?" God provides redemptive elements in our walk with Him to lessen the pain of regrets. I have seen people in their 80s and 90s experience a baptism of love and have an orphan spirit healed. "I just didn't know . . . ," they say. But they know now, and they see redemption in the fact that they have arrived at a place that can become a starting point for the next generation. Even just getting there is redemptive and a blessing to those still to come. Even a great-grandfather can begin to live from sonship.

David never found the peace he was looking for, but his son got to establish peace in the next generation. There is power in running this leg of the race for those who will take the baton from us and go further. The great cloud of witnesses still rejoices in that fact (Hebrews 12:1). When you get into that place of sonship or daughtership, your focus is no longer on what is lacking—or on what you've missed. It's on what you have. The Father's living room is not a place of insufficiency. It is a place to be thankful for everything you have been able to experience and for what is still yet to come.

It took me awhile to get to where I am, but generations could only dream of experiencing even a minute of what you and I can experience now. We have the opportunity now to see the Father's face, walk under an open heaven, and host the presence of the Dove. However long it took to get there, it is always worth the journey.

CHAPTER SIXTEEN
DEVOTIONAL
Living in a Kingdom Culture

Throughout this book there has been a strong emphasis on sonship. Oftentimes we take on other "ships" before we are fully formed sons or daughters. When this happens, it's easy to get shipwrecked. If you've ever been shipwrecked you know what a difficult and scary place that can be. The extreme challenges of life can make you feel like you are alone in a vast ocean with no rescue in sight. In reality, that's a Chair 2 feeling. From Chair 1, we know God is always with us, and so is the rest of His family. In community we thrive and grow, eventually becoming spiritual mothers and fathers who sow into the next generation. However, you can't be a parent until you've been a son or daughter. Sonship comes first. If you have fallen out of Chair 1 and are struggling to get back in, know that it is never too late with God. His timing is perfect; nothing is ever wasted with Him, and everything builds on the journey with Him. Instead of focusing on what you have missed, focus on what you have in the Father's living room, the place of absolute and complete sufficiency.

FOCUS AREAS

Chair 1 Living:

» Marriage – we don't compete; we complete.
» Business – you represent the core values of the Trinity in the workplace.
» Church – Chair 1 churches represent the Kingdom family in such a way as to become irresistible invitations for and authentic voices in the community.

REFLECTION

Take some time alone with God today. Step into His living room. Pull up Chair 1 in the presence of the Father. Let Him wrap His arms of love around you and draw you close, into the place reserved for beloved sons and daughters. Give Him all your "ships" and settle into the place of sonship marked with your name. Allow Him to wash away your regrets and your fears and doubts with His magnificent, loving presence. And then, just rest.

Part Four Summary Reflection:
DESTINY

What Am I Called to Do?

In chapter 12 we looked at what it means to be part of Papa's family, on a mission with God, living out our destiny over the course of a lifetime. This kind of Kingdom living requires seasons of preparation – training for reigning. In the course of our training, it's good to be able to define our mission so we can be faithful to our calling. Chapter 13 helps focus us on what is involved in being part of God's family, teaching us about the necessity of humility, vulnerability and relationship, and that God is there to equip us for every challenge. Chapter 14 tackles the topic of being change agents in the culture, living as sons and daughters of glory, with a servant's towel over our arm, as we learn the rhythm of love, power and wisdom. Chapter 15 highlights reformation and revival, both historically and in the present day, encouraging us to see how our destiny is connected to those who came before us, and those who are coming after us. Chapter 16 concludes the book with a refocus on the importance of sonship, encouraging us to press on from that place of rest in the Father's living room, where we can experience absolute and complete sufficiency.

ACTIVATION

» Congratulations! You have just completed an amazing time of learning and pressing in to who you are, who God is, what is available to you, and what you are called to do. The godly, biblical knowledge that you have gained should be something you carry with you, there to equip, encourage and empower you as you dream with God. You are a beloved member of God's family and He loves you with an everlasting love. Be encouraged to take what you have learned and go into your spheres of influence today, partnering with God to bring heaven to earth. Don't wait! He will be there with you at every turn. God will walk with you through the valleys to the mountaintops and back again. When you find yourself becoming restless, ask the Father, "Which chair am I sitting in?" Remember, you are a resting place for the Dove, with the ring of identity, the robe of righteousness, and the sandals of peace. He trusts you with the family inheritance. It's time to rule and reign with Papa God.

PRAYER

My prayer for each of you is that your inner and outer world will be forever changed; that you will never forget who you are; that you will know the height, depth, width, and breadth of the Father's love, see His face, hear His voice, experience His presence, and enjoy His pleasure every day; and that you will receive every ounce of your inheritance and step into every inch of the destiny He has planned for you.

Leif Hetland

APPENDIX

POSITIONED TO REIGN

We are called to reign from a position of rest in and with our Father. When we are in Chair 1 we are seated in our rightful place where we understand who we are, where we are, what we have and what we are called to do. The following table provides a clear comparison between Chair 1 and Chair 2.

Chair 1	Chair 2
Kingdom of God	Kingdom of self
Love-based	Fear-based
Rooted in spirit of sonship	Rooted in orphan spirit
Experiences the Dove's habitation	Experiences the Dove's visitation
Be/Have/Do	Do/Have/Be
Prioritizes identity and intimacy over inheritance and destiny	Prioritizes inheritance and destiny over identity and intimacy
Wants to bring heaven to earth	Wants to get from earth to heaven
Lives *from* God	Lives *for* God
The believer's touch cleanses the world	The world's touch corrupts the believer
Sets the temperature like a thermostat	Measures the temperature like a thermometer
Treats people according to their destiny	Treats people according to their history
Influences the world	Influenced by the world
Confident in hearing God's voice	Afraid of being misled
God's pleasure without performing	Pressure to perform
At rest	Restless